You are Innocent!

God's foundation for meaningful friendship

Rudi Louw

Copyright © 2013 Rudi Louw Publishing

("The Age of Innocence" revised edition)

All rights reserved solely by the author. No part of this book may be reproduced in any form without the permission of the author.

Most Scripture quotations are from the Revised Standard Version, Holy Bible, Thomas Nelson Publishers. Copyright © 1983 by Thomas Nelson, Inc.

Some Scripture quotations are from the New King James Version, Holy Bible, Thomas Nelson Publishers. Copyright © 1983 by Thomas Nelson, Inc.

All Scripture quotations not taken from the RSV and NKJV are a literal translation of the Scriptures.

The Holy Scriptures are just that, HOLY. Statements enclosed in brackets were inserted into Scripture quotations to add emphasis or clarify the meaning of what is being said in those scriptures. The integrity of God's Word to man was not compromised in any way. Due care and diligence was cautiously exercised to keep the Word of Truth intact.

For example, the apostle Paul said in his second letter to Timothy in chapter three verse sixteen that:

"All Scripture is given by inspiration of God (literally God breathed) and is profitable for doctrine, for reproof, for correction, for instruction **in righteousness**,"

Contents

The marvel of the Holy Bible

1. The theme and inspired thought of Scripture continues uninterrupted.

It took *1,500 years* to compile the Holy Bible, involving *more than 40 different authors*, yet the theme and inspired thought of Scripture continues *uninterrupted*, from author to author, from beginning till end.

2. Absence of mythical stories:

Compare philosophies and theories about creation in the Middle East, Europe, Asia, Africa and Latin America, and you will find mythical scenarios; gods feuding with and cutting up other gods to form the heavens and the earth. In ancient Greek mythology, the Greeks see Atlas carrying the earth on his shoulders. In India, Hindus believe 8 elephants carry the earth on their backs.

But in contrast, Job, the oldest book in the Holy Bible, declares that *God suspends the earth 'on nothing.'* (Job 26:7)

This was said millennia before Isaac Newton discovered the invisible laws of gravity that delicately balance every planet and sun in its individual circuit.

In contrast to every other ancient attempt to give a creation account, *the Holy Bible pictures the creation of the earth in a very scientific manner.*

In Gen 1 for instance, the continents are lifted from the seas, and then vegetation is created and later, animal life, all reproducing *'according to its own kind,'* **thus recognising the fixed genetic laws.** Finally, we have the creation of man and woman, *all done by God in a dignified and proper manner, without mythological adornments.*

The rest of the Holy Bible follows suite.

The narratives are **true historical documents**, *faithfully reflecting society and culture* **as history and archaeology would discover them thousands of years later. Not only is the Holy Bible historically accurate, it is also reliable when it deals with scientific subjects.**

It was not written as a textbook on history, science, mathematics or medicine, *yet,*

when its writers touch on these subjects, they often state facts that scientific advancement would not reveal or even consider until thousands of years later.

While many have doubted the accuracy of the Holy Bible, time and continued research have consistently demonstrated that the Word of God is better informed than its critics.

3. The Holy Bible is intact.

Of all the ancient works of substantial size, the Holy Bible against all odds and expectations survives intact.

Compared with other ancient writings, the Holy Bible has more manuscripts as evidence to support it than any ten pieces of classical literature combined!

The plays of William Shakespeare, for instance, were written about four hundred years ago, and written after the invention of the printing press.

Many of his original words have been lost in numerous sections, *yet the Holy Bible's uncanny preservation has weathered thousands of years of wars, contradictions, persecutions, fires and invasions.*

*Jewish scribes, **like no other manuscript has ever been preserved**, preserved the Holy Bible's Old Covenant text through centuries. **They kept tabs on every letter, syllable, word and paragraph**.*

*They continued from generation to generation to appoint and train special classes of men within their culture, **whose sole duty it was to preserve and transmit these documents, <u>with perfect accuracy and fidelity</u>**.*

Who ever bothered to count the letters, syllables, or words of Plato, Aristotle or Seneca for that matter?

When it comes to the New Testament, the actual number of preserved manuscripts is so great that it becomes overwhelming.

There are more than 5,680 Greek manuscripts, more than 10,000 Latin Vulgate and at least 9,300 other versions; there exist a further 25,000 manuscript copies of portions of the New Testament.

No other document of antiquity even begins to approach such numbers. The closest in comparison is Homer's <u>Iliad</u> with only 643 manuscripts. The first complete work of Homer only dates back to the 13th century.

4. In dealing with time, the Holy Bible accurately foretells what will happen ahead of time, with unmatched results.

No other ancient work even begins to attempt this.

Other books claim divine inspiration, such as the Koran, the Book of Mormon, and parts of the Veda. *But none of these books contains predictive foretelling.*

This one fact we know for certain and it is undeniable: *While microscopic scrutiny would show up the imperfections, blemishes and defects of any work of man, <u>it magnifies the beauties and perfection of God</u>, just as every flower displays in accurate detail, the reflection and perfection of beauty, <u>so does the Word of Truth when it is scrutinized</u>.*

Historian, Philip Schaff wrote:

'…Without money and weapons, Jesus the Christ conquered more millions than Alexander, Caesar, Mohammed and Napoleon. Without science and learning, He (Jesus the Christ) shed more light on things human and divine than all philosophers and scholars combined. Without the eloquence of schools, He (Jesus the Christ) spoke such words of life

*as was never spoken before or since and produced effects, which lie beyond the reach of orator or poet. Without writing a single line, He (Jesus the Christ) set more pens in motion, and furnished themes for more sermons, orations, discussions, learned volumes, works of art, and songs of praise, **than the whole army of great men of ancient and modern times combined.**'* (The person of Christ p33. 1913)

Today, there are literally billions of Bibles in more than 2,000 languages, *isn't it about time you find out what it really has to say?*

Hey listen, the Holy Bible is all about Jesus, the Messiah, the Christ ...*and everything about Jesus Christ is really about YOU!!*

Study Tips:

Read 2Corinthians 5:14, 16, 18, 19, and 21. In the light of these scriptures, it should be obvious that if you want to study the Holy Bible *you should study it in the light of mankind's Redemption!*

Daily feed on Redemption Realities, especially Romans 1 through 8, Ephesians, Colossians, Galatians, 1Peter 1, 2Peter 1, James 1, 1 and 2Corinthians, and the book of Acts.

Acknowledgment

I want to acknowledge and thank one of my mentors in the faith, Francois du Toit, for blessing and impacting my life with revelation knowledge.

The portion on *"The marvel of the Holy Bible"* was borrowed from his website: http://www.mirrorword.net/ as students so often feel they have a right to do with things that come from teachers they respect. Just as Galatians 6:6 says: *"Let him who is taught the Word **share in all good things** with him who teaches."*

To all our many dear friends and our precious family whom we love, and to those who helped me with this project,

...but especially to my sweet wife, Carmen:

For all your love and support,

THANK YOU!

Foreword

Thank you for taking the time to read this book.

Let me start by saying that I am thoroughly addicted to my Daddy's point of reference; His love and eternal opinion of me; I am in love with Jesus Christ, *and that is enough for me!*

The love of God is so much more than a doctrine, a philosophy, or a theory; it is so much more and goes so much deeper than knowledge; it way surpasses knowledge.

We *are talking heart language here,*

...therefore this book was not written to impress intellectuals with knowledge and philosophy, theologians with theories and doctrine, nor English majors with grammar and spelling for that matter, *so if you come up with any other definitions, opposing references or find any language inaccuracies,* **please do not use it to disqualify Love's own message I bring to you in this book**.

I write **to impact people's hearts**;

...to make them see the mysteries that have been hidden in Father God's heart, concerning Christ Jesus, and really, **concerning THEM**, so as to arrest their conscience with it **that I**

may introduce them to their original design, and to their true selves; and *present them to themselves perfect in Christ Jesus,* and *set them apart unto Him in love,* as a chaste virgin,

"...for by Him all things were created... All things were created through Him and for Him. And He is before all things

(He has been in existence from the beginning. He has always been in existence and holds the place of pre-eminence over everything; He is the Prince of LIFE Himself), *and in Him all things consist*

(...everything in creation is still working according to its design and is held together in Him; *in His power proceeding from His heart of love.*

Everything and everyone find their place of existence; their function and purpose; their place of significance; their precise reason for being; *their exact home and belonging, in Him who loves them and gave Himself to them)."* Colossians 1:16 & 17

We are dealing with the biggest romance of the ages here!

...therefore, this book cannot be read as you would read a novel, casually. It is not a cleverly devised myth or fable. **It contains revelation and *truth* into some things you may or may not have considered before.**

It is not blasphemy or error. *It is the TRUTH of God, ultimate TRUTH, and therefore has direct bearing upon YOUR life,* the Word, and the Spirit is my witness *to the reality of these things!*

I challenge you, be like the people of Berea the apostle Paul ministered to in Acts 17:11. *Open yourself up to study the revelation contained in this book,* but be forewarned, do not become guilty of the sins of the Pharisees, **or you to will miss out on the depth of fulfillment God Himself, who is LOVE, want to give you**.

(Jesus said of the Pharisees and Sadducees, *"…they strain out every little gnat, BUT swallow whole camels."* What He meant by that is that *some people **seem** to have it all together when it comes to doctrine, and they love to argue. It makes them feel important, but it is nothing other than EMPTY religious and intellectual pride. They know the Scriptures in and out, and YET they are still so IGNORANT about REAL TRUTH that is only found in LOVE; they are still so indifferent towards the things that MATTERS MOST.* They are always arguing over the use of every little jot and tittle and the meaning and interpretation of every word of Scripture.

The exact thing they accuse everyone else of doing though; *the precise thing they judge everyone else for,* they are actually doing themselves. **They often utterly misinterpret and twist what is being said, making a big**

deal of insignificant things, *while obscuring or weakening God's real truth; the truth of His LOVE.*

They are always majoring on minors because they do not understand the heart of God, and *therefore, they constantly miss the whole point of the message*.)

Paul himself said it so beautifully:

*"...the letter kills but **the Spirit BRINGS LIFE**; "*

*"...knowledge puffs up, but **LOVE EDIFIES** (**encourages and builds up**)."*

I say again: *Allow yourself to get caught up in the revelation I am about to share. Open yourself up to study the insight contained in this book.* Do not merely have a desire to gain knowledge, but study it with anticipation to hear from Father God for yourself, in order to encounter Him through His Word and to embrace the truth, *so that you may know and believe that God LOVES you and that He has made you INNOCENT and ACCEPTED you in the Beloved* (in Jesus).

The whole purpose of you knowing and believing this reality *is for you to get so caught up in it **that you to may receive from LOVE, a genuine impartation of INNOCENCE and LIFE.***

This revelation contains within it the voice and call of LOVE Himself to every human being on the face of this earth. If you take heed to it, it is custom designed and guaranteed to alter and enrich your life forever!

That which was from the beginning,

which we have heard
(with our spiritual ears),
which we have seen
(with our spiritual eyes),
which we have looked upon
(beheld, focused our attention upon),
and which our hands have also handled **(which we have also experienced)**,
concerning the Word of Life,
we declare to you,

that you also may have this
fellowship with us;

and truly our fellowship is with
the Father
and with His Son Jesus Christ.

And these things we write to you
that your joy may be full.

~ 1 John 1:1-4

Prayer

Father, as we bow our hearts before you now, we recognize again that your voice is in your Word, and that we're not just facing an empty page, but Father, *we're looking into your heart* as we read the Holy Scriptures.

I thank you that *You have unveiled Your heart to us,* Lord.

I thank you that we're not busy with dogmatic principle and old religious ideas, but Father, *we're in fellowship with Your heartbeat as we study what is revealed to us in the incarnation of Your Son; in His life, death, burial, resurrection, and ascension,* **written about in the Scriptures,**

…and I thank you that, as I write and we communicate *heart to heart* right now, that the Holy Spirit will take these words and sharpen them and cut into our hearts Lord, and imprint in our spirits **that Word of Truth that is LIFE indeed,** in Jesus' name.

Thank you Lord that Your Word will not return to You void.

Thank you that You're not just speaking, Father, vain and empty words and clichés, but you're speaking into our lives **that Word that**

will liberate; that Word that will anoint us; that Word that will equip us with enough love;

…with TRUE LOVE,

…to DO **the work of loving and ministering to others.**

In Jesus' name.

Amen.

Chapter 1

God is at work within you

In writing this book, I want to communicate and speak to you *heart to heart* on the subject of *innocence.*

It is my desire for all of us together to see the importance and value of innocence when it comes to relationship, friendship and fellowship.

I believe that many of us have come to discover that religion without relationship, without friendship, without fellowship is totally void and empty.

The quality, the essence of what we have in Christianity...

(I am not talking about the Christian religion here.

I do not like calling what we have; RELIGION.

True Christianity is not a religion!

Jesus Christ did not come to start another religion as if there aren't enough religions in the world already.

Jesus' mission was not to start the Christian religion.

His mandate was not to give us a new calendar.

The western calendar merely testifies to the fact that 2013 years ago the creator of the universe came to visit the planet.

...He came to visit His own, camouflaged in a human body, to redeem and rescue lost humanity!

Jesus' mission wasn't to come and start His own rival synagogue system, called *"The Church."*

...He didn't come to start a little organization, called, whatever we want to banner ourselves as.

His mandate was to reveal and redeem the original blueprint of our design!

His mandate was to be an exact expression of the invisible God; to reveal Him, *and at the same time to reveal our true identity to us!*

He didn't come with yet another moral code; another set of moral do's and don'ts;

He didn't come to win protest votes against Moses, Mohamed, Buddha, Confucius and all the rest, and to say: *'Hey, vote for Me! Vote for Me! Vote for Me! Hey, choose Me please!'*

He didn't come with yet another cause to support; He didn't come to contest His cause!

He didn't come to compete with Moses, Mohamed, Buddha, Confucius and all the rest.

No, *He came to reveal; He came to unveil!*

He came to redeem and restore the image and likeness of God in man.

...He came to reconcile Daddy God's kids back unto Him,

...that means us, me and YOU,

While He was being gossiped about in the religious circles, *the sinners, the worst of them, felt irresistibly attracted to Him.*

Why?

A compromised standard?

'Ten out of ten is impossible, so now you can just stick to five, and it'll be okay?'

No!

He didn't come to compromise anything.

He didn't come with more rules either, even stricter ones.

No, *He didn't bother with rules; **He didn't bother to adjust the rules***…

He came to reveal the glory; *that original authentic glory!*

He came to restore and reestablish us, YOU included, in blameless innocence and righteousness! *That is why He came.*)

…what we have in True Christianity, *the quality of it, the essence of it* is found, **not in being religious,** *but in intimate fellowship and friendship with God.*

God desires that friendship, that fellowship to be a quality one.

You see there are many kinds of relationships in the world, but most of them are on very shaky ground.

God desires our relationship with Him to be an intimate, quality relationship, a totally radiant, transparent relationship, measured by innocence.

Jesus said in Matthew 18:3,

3 *"…unless you are converted and become as little children, you will by no means enter the kingdom of Heaven"* NKJV

He was not talking about going to Heaven one day.

He was talking about *entering the kingdom of God within us;* that spirit dimension, that realm of relationship with God, *in the Holy Spirit.*

Luke 18:17

17 *"Assuredly, I say to you, whoever does not* **receive** *the kingdom of God* **<u>as a little child</u>** **will by no means enter it***." NKJV

The kingdom of God is within us. It is righteousness peace and joy, in the Holy Spirit. (Luke 17:20, 21; Romans 14:17)

Obviously, those that do enter the kingdom of God *within them,* and abide there in a relationship with the Holy Spirit; in friendship and fellowship with God, *will also one day end up in heaven.*

I say again:

God desires our relationship with Him to be measured by child-like faith and trust,

God desires our relationship with Him to be an intimate, vibrant, quality relationship, a totally radiant, transparent relationship,

...measured by child-like innocence.

Relationship that springs from and is founded *upon innocence* takes on a certain *thoroughly satisfying quality.*

*...*absolute satisfaction!

I truly believe that *innocence* measures <u>the quality</u> of our relationship.

Let's look at Philippians chapter 2.

Philippians 2:12-16

12 *"Therefore, my beloved, as you have always obeyed, not as in my presence only, but now much more in my absence, **work out your own salvation** with fear and trembling; "*

13 ***"for it is God who works in you both to will and to do His good pleasure"***

14 *"Do all things without murmuring and disputing* (grumbling, complaining, reasoning and arguing),*"*

15 ***"that you may become blameless and harmless** (or innocent)**, children of God without fault** (without blemish) **in the midst of a crooked and perverse generation, among whom you shine as lights in the world***,"*

16 *"**holding fast the Word of life,** so that I may rejoice in the day of Christ, that I have not run in vain, or labored in vain"* NKJV

The NASV (New American Standard Version) says:

Philippians 2:13

13 *"...**For God is at work within you**..."*

*"...**For God IS at work within you**..."* is the greatest factor of your life.

Let me say it another way:

The greatest factor, the greatest truth about you, is the work of God; the workmanship of God within you.

Therefore, the greatest factor, the greatest truth about you, as a believer, is the working of God within you.

You see, before **you heard and received the Gospel of grace, the Word of Truth,** your life was qualified by your education, by your personality, by your talent, by whom you knew and how prominent you were in the natural,

...but now there's a new qualification to our lives, because,

2Corinthians 5:17

17 *"...if any man is in Christ Jesus, he's a new creature; the old things have passed away..."*

Paul says in another place that,

'Whatever gain I had I count it as loss.'

He says that,

'I could boast in the flesh, I have much reason to try and promote myself because of my secular and religious education, because of my secular and religious background and my social stand and my zeal.'

He says,

'But all those things that were gain; that were so valuable to me; that gave me such prominence in life; '

He says,

'I count them as refuse; I count them as dung.'

He says,

*'I've discovered a new gain and **that gain is in the excellence of the knowledge of Jesus,** that revelation that God shone forth in my heart when He revealed His Son to me, **and in me,** and that revelation **became the treasure** in this earthen vessel.'*

He says,

*'Now I boast **in that treasure,** I glory **in the knowledge that I am accepted in the Beloved,** that **I am a partaker of the Divine nature,** I glory in that **knowledge that Christ is in me,** I glory in the knowledge that Jesus **is within me**.'*

So the greatest factor of our lives is related to God's working within us.

It is not related to anything in the natural.

*'We put no confidence in the flesh, but **our confidence is based upon the working of God within us**'* says Paul.

I praise God for that work; that workmanship; that working, amen?!

So Paul writes here to the Philippians, and he says in verse 13:

Philippians 2:13

13 *"...**For <u>God is at work within you</u>**..."*

I mean I could just stop writing, and we can just read that right now and say hallelujah, let's just sit back and for the next 24 hours enjoy meditating on that one *...on the working of God **within us***

...experiencing and treasuring that working!

...treasuring that work; His workmanship in us!

How do we encourage that working, how do we treasure that work, how do we stimulate that working?

You know, because it is possible for you to quench that working.

It's possible for you *to neutralize,* **through your attitude, and your reaction, and your response, and your doubt and double-mindedness,** *to interfere with the working of God within you.*

So Paul knows that, and he is determined to encourage us in saying:

"Do all things **without murmuring and disputing** (grumbling, complaining, reasoning and arguing against God, in doubt and unbelief),*"*

He says, hey listen, *"...**God is at work <u>within you</u>**...*"

*"<u>**GOD**</u> **is at work** within you..."*

That means God is responsible for what *He* has produced in your life.

God is not responsible for what the devil has produced in your life!

God is not responsible for what circumstances have produced in your life!

God is not responsible for what doubt and unbelief have produced in your life!

God is responsible for what *He's* produced in your life.

God is only responsible for what *He through faith impartation* has produced in your life!

God is only responsible for what *accurate faith* has produced in your life!

Would you agree with me that God is a responsible God?

God takes His responsibility very seriously.

God is responsible for what *He's* produced in your life.

God is responsible *for every good thing that is within you* in Christ Jesus.

Philippians 2:13,

*"…God is at work within you, **both to will and to do, both to will and to work His good pleasure…"***

You see in verse 12 he says:

Philippians 2:12,

12 *"**Work out** your own salvation…"*

So we think:

'Oh, now how am I going to do that?'

*'How am I going to "**work out**" my own salvation?'*

*'I mean my old background testifies of my vain attempts to try and be a better Christian, to try and be a better person. You know, and I follow the next set of rules and the next philosophy and the next idea, **and I just come to the end of myself**.'*

And now Paul says here:

Philippians 2:12

12 *"**Work out your own salvation**…"*

'I thought God will do it all.'

He says:

Philippians 2:12

12 *"**<u>Work out</u>** your own salvation… **for God is at work within you**."*

The meaning in the Greek of the phrase,

34

*"**work out** your own salvation"* is:

To come to a mathematical conclusion about your salvation

In other words,

Come to the same mathematical conclusion, *the same logical conclusion as God* concerning your salvation.

My friends that is the meaning of faith!

...*come into agreement with God* about your salvation

*"...**for God is at work within you**."*

That means,

I cannot afford to come to the wrong conclusion concerning my salvation, *for God is at work within me.*

12 *"**Work out** your own salvation... **for God is at work within you**."*

We can work out our own salvation; *we can enter into* our salvation; <u>we can give expression to</u> that salvation BECAUSE God is at work within us.

You see, *everything we enjoy* in the New Covenant *is directly related to faith; it is directly related to that working of God within us.*

When Paul prays for us in Ephesians chapter 3, he says:

Ephesians 3:16,

16 *'I pray that you'd "**be strengthened with might <u>by His Spirit</u>** in the inner man…'*

In other words, and I paraphrase:

Ephesians 3:16-20,

*"…that **God will strengthen your inner man** with might, **working within you**, far abundantly above all that you can ask or think… …**working within you that truth**…"*

And now, He says here in verse 14 of Philippians chapter 2:

Philippians 2:14,

14 *"Do all things without grumbling **or questioning**."*

Why would we grumble or question?

I believe grumbling and questioning *is not the fruit of faith*,

…<u>it's not the fruit of spiritual knowledge</u>,

…it's the fruit of natural knowledge.

You see God sometimes works things in our lives, *and He is challenging us with truth,* and suddenly we begin to question God and we want to resist Him and it's not so comfortable anymore, and we begin to question and grumble and mumble,

…and God says:

*'Hey listen, just be quiet and believe that I'm the one speaking in your heart; that **I'm working within you**, even though you might not feel like it's working for you, or you may not **see it** right now, **just enjoy My truth, just yield in your heart and embrace My working within you, just rest in Me,** just rest in the fact that I am working within you, just rest in that.'*

*'Don't try and work it out with your think-tank, just rest in Me; **just trust in Me,** because **I'm** working within you, **I am working within <u>you</u>**.'*

It's the greatest liberty that I could ever enjoy, the fact that **God is at this moment working within me**.

This is His workshop, this inner-man, this heart, this inside here. It's not just stomach juices and things building my body, but *in my spirit, in my inner-man God the Holy Spirit is quickening me.*

He's quickening my spirit. He's quickening me personally; *waking me up to His reality; to His **working** within me.*

He is working within me!

…He's even quickening my mortal body *by that interaction within me;* within my spirit.

So the Word says:

Philippians 2:14-15,

14 *"Don't let questionings and grumbling* **interrupt truth, interrupt that working**…"

15 *"***so that <u>you</u> may be <u>blameless</u>**…"*

Now God is speaking about **you** okay?

Not just the Philippians, but **<u>you</u>**!!

Philippians 2:15

15 *"so that* **<u>YOU</u>** *may be* **<u>blameless and innocent</u>**, *children of God,* **<u>without blemish</u>**…"

And now immediately we think: *'Well, that's one day in Heaven, you know. Praise God, one day in Heaven it'll be all over; we're going to be blameless, innocent, children of God, without blemish…'*

And then we hear Paul say…

Philippians 2:15,

15 *"...here in the midst of a crooked and perverse generation..."*

And we think: *'Hey Paul, wait a minute man, you don't know what it looks like in the year 2013, especially here towards the end.'*

Philippians 2:15

15 *"...In the midst of a crooked and perverse generation among whom you shine as lights in the world..."*

Where are we going to get that light from?

From His working within us you see!

So the *"working out"* **of my salvation is just the shining part.**

It's just *the fruit;* ***the displaying*** **of the working** *of His grace* **within me; the working** *of His love and His truth* **in my inner-man; the working** *of His Word of Life* **within me; the working** *of His faith and of His power* **within my spirit.**

You see the key is in verse 16:

Philippians 2:16,

16 *"...Holding fast to the Word of life..."*

The truth is,

The moment _fellowship_ with the truth of redemption, _fellowship with the Word of life_ is interrupted ...the working of God in your inner-man is also interrupted.

It's like a factory. I mean, you can have the factory all set up out there with all the machinery and all the works, _but as soon as you run out of material the factory can no longer produce._

Please listen to me: The Holy Spirit cannot produce anything in your life without the Word of life, whether that Word comes through people or the Scriptures directly.

_It's that _holding fast_ to the Word _that brings His working; His LIFE_, into your inner-man._

Philippians 2:16

16 _"Holding fast to the Word..."_

"Holding fast" again speaks of _an attitude of your heart._

It means I am no longer casual about the Word of God, _but I'm holding it fast, I'm embracing it_ in my inner-man, _I'm drawing from its life_, being _energized by it,_

...and I'm allowing the Holy Spirit _to impart the faith of God, to feed me_ with His truth and love, _to take every Word and work it into my inner-man,_

40

*...and **build that love and that truth and that faith into my spirit,***

*...and **build it into my mind,***

*...**renewing the spirit of my mind,***

*...**so that my whole life can shine forth in the midst of** this crooked dark world.*

Praise God!

Philippians 2:16

16 *"...**Holding fast** to the **Word of life** so that in the day of Christ I may be pleased that I did not run in vain or labor in vain."*

Can you see that God desires *a quality relationship,* quality of fellowship with us?

God truly does desire a quality relationship, *a blameless innocent fellowship* with us; a relationship **of absolute innocence**, *nothing standing between us, no hindrances, nothing there **to jeopardize that fellowship and diminish it in value.***

41

Chapter 2

The ugly story of sin

In the Scriptures, we have a reference in Genesis where God made Adam and Eve, and that *they enjoyed a dispensation of* **absolute innocence**.

I mean, when Adam and Eve **walked with God enjoying that intimate fellowship** *they were guilt-free;*

There was no consciousness within them *of any form of guilt, of any form of disappointment, of any form of fear or inferiority.*

They were only <u>conscious</u> of an absolute enjoyment, the absolute bliss of walking with God.

Hey THAT is quality!

*...***totally transparent, totally <u>innocent</u>, no hindrances, nothing to hide, no knowledge of evil, no knowledge of guilt, no knowledge of inferiority, of weakness or failure, no knowledge of bad, but just an absolute enjoyment and a knowledge; <u>a strong</u>**

witness; _a strong resonance and reflection_ _of the life of God_ _within them_.

God made them _in His own image and likeness,_ **and their walk with God was just** _a_ **strong mutual witness in their spirits; a resonance, a feed-back, a reflection** of _that absolute unity; that absolute harmony,_ being _totally united_ **with their Maker.**

They were enjoying **a** _righteousness_ and **an** **innocence** _that was a result_ of what they were made to be; _it was the essence of their true selves; of their true identity;_ **they were made to be that; they were made to be righteous, they were made to be innocent; it was what they were made for.**

And we know the ugly story of sin, how it came to mar and destroy _that innocence, that righteousness,_ how it introduced to them _the knowledge of evil_

...and they began to _know_ evil, they began to know **the fruit** of evil, they began to _know_ that death, **that separation, that guilt** _that caused them to lose that righteousness, that innocence, and_ **hide away from** _the presence of God..._

...**and throughout the ages man's number one need is** _to come again_ **into a relationship of** _innocence,_ **a relationship of** _righteousness_ **with God**.

44

In many Christian religious circles the word *"righteousness"* is interpreted to mean: **right standing; to have right standing; or to be in right standing with God** and, therefore, it is quite often seen in a legalistic light, to have *everything* to do with *right conduct,* and it is therefore used most of the time to refer to ones *conduct.*

It is interpreted to mean that *'I am in right standing with God, because of my good conduct; because* **my conduct lines up with what is required of me; I am in right standing with God because of my obedience,***'* in other words it has everything to do with *upholding a moral standard.*

In actuality the word, *"righteousness"* does not speak really of conduct but *something much greater!*

Right conduct *is merely* **the fruit of** *"righteousness."*

"Righteousness" has more to do with **the root** than *the fruit.*

It has more to do with our authentic original design; with our true identity;

Our righteous conduct is an outflow of that identity of *"righteousness."*

"Righteousness" is therefore more about **right-being,** and **right-believing,** than right-doing.

45

Our righteous life is *merely the by-product of our "righteousness."*

The Hebrew word for *"righteousness"* is the word TZADOK, which refers to *the wooden beam in a scale of balances.*

It is both the balancing beam and the pivotal point of the balance

...thus, the whole balance hangs on it and depends on it.

It has everything to do with *balancing out the equation,* or the *accuracy of the equation.*

Our modern word, *'righteousness'* actually comes from an old Anglo Saxon word meaning: *'right-wise-ness;'*

...to be wise concerning that which is right, or true, or accurate

The etymological essence of the word, *"righteousness"* in its root form, DIKE, *implies the idea of, two parties finding likeness in each other,*

...with no interference of any sense of blame, guilt or inferiority.

When Adam lost the glory of God (Hebrew, KABOD, *weight; the consciousness, the truth of God's likeness and image*)...

...the law then came and **proved** that *no amount of good works* (or right conduct) *could balance the scale again.*

Only faith, only the truth restored, only the restored consciousness of God's image and likeness, of innocence, could balance the scale again!

Grace; the work of redemption; the gospel *reveals how God redeemed, and restored, His image and likeness again in human form;*

Now the scale is perfectly balanced again in Christ!

You can go and research how throughout the ages every religion has one thing in common:

...a desperate desire for man to obtain innocence, to obtain justification, to obtain righteousness, to obtain again a right standing towards Deity

...because there is a God sized hole in every man's heart,

...and there is something else that also haunts every man, and it's the fear of death.

That fear challenges every human being. It challenges them. It says to them all the time:

'Your life can be cut short, just like that, in a twinkling of an eye, in a snap of the finger, in a moment of time, then what will happen to you, then what will you have and where will you be?'

And so, desperately man's heart cries out for some security that he can anchor and secure and found himself upon.

That's why, in the Scriptures we begin to see God introduce through the Old Covenant *a righteousness of the Law.*

And God said:

'This is My Commandment, this is My Law, this is the blessing that I link to that Law, and this is the curse **that is inevitably linked to that Law**.'

And man began to strive, through obedience to the Law, *to obtain some form of righteousness, some form of innocence,* **but only to fail again,**

...and every year there would be *another* sacrifice required.

In every sacrifice, man was just displaying *his fruitless attempts to enjoy innocence with God.*

Every sacrifice that man brought, every sacrifice, *he had to hang his head in shame and guilt, recognizing that he is guilty,*

…that he has failed God,

…recognizing that this animal is standing in *as his substitute* **to take his guilt**

But, thank God, those sacrifices were pointing *towards a day*,

…**they were pointing *towards a person* that would come to unequivocally restore man in absolute righteousness and total innocence.**

Now we need to appreciate that *God's working within us* is to produce *an absolute blameless innocence*,

…**because the quality of our relationship is measured *by that innocence***

When I use the word, *innocence, I am referring to the kind of warmth and acceptance true love alone can bring into a relationship.*

I am talking about true righteousness;

I am talking about *the genuineness, blamelessness, and transparency I am afforded, and enjoy intimately, by the purity of that love.*

In other words, *I can enjoy guiltlessness in that relationship*,

…meaning, *I can be transparent,*

I no longer feel the need to hide anything,

…*in the light of that acceptance, I enjoy such intimacy and innocence,* I no longer have anything to hide any more, *I am truly free, I have nothing to hide,*

I become radiant and transparent.

…and *because I treasure that intimate freedom* I refuse to jeopardize the quality of our relationship, in fact,

I keep on nurturing and cultivating it.

Ephesians 1:6

6 *"…to the praise* (the marvel, the appreciation, the treasuring) *of the glory of His grace, by which He made us accepted in the Beloved"*

It's *impossible* to enjoy the presence of God with a consciousness of sin!

I can never totally enjoy praise or worship, or any real move of the Spirit, *while there's a consciousness within me of my own failure, my own unworthiness, of my own weakness and my own guilt.*

So I need to understand that God has made provision for a total release as far as my guilt is concerned,

Because He desires to bring me back *into a place of mutual witness,* of mutual RECOGNITION;

…where I am again embraced in the presence of God

…and I know that God recognizes me and that I am reckoned by Him, and I reckon Him…

…and there's a constant flow of witness between us,

…of acceptance, of recognition, of companionship,

…because of that righteousness!

I say again,

I need to understand that <u>God has made provision for a total release as far as my guilt is concerned</u>,

Because He desires to bring me back into a place where I am again embraced in His presence,

…<u>a relationship of mutual recognition; of mutual treasuring; of mutual worth; of mutual respect and honor and value and love</u>

And so, in Hebrews chapter 10, we have a beautiful scripture that perhaps stands out as the climax of the revelation of the New Testament.

I believe that verse 19 and what follows immediately there is perhaps the whole crux of the New Covenant.

Chapter 3

True unity versus the shallowness of tolerance

Hebrews 10:19-22

19 *"Therefore brethren,* **since we have confidence** to enter the sanctuary by the blood of Jesus*,"*

20 *"***by the new and living way, which He opened for us** *through the curtain, that is through his flesh,"*

21 *"and since we have a great priest over the house of God"*

22 *"***let us draw near** *with a true heart;* **in full assurance of faith, with our hearts sprinkled clean** (through the blood and through the truth of redemption) ***from an evil conscience* and our bodies washed** **(sanctified, set apart)** *with pure water* (the water; the influence of the Spirit of Truth)…"*

*"…***our bodies washed** *with pure water…"*

"… our **hearts cleansed** *from an evil* **conscience**…"*

…no memory, no thought, no suspicion left in my mind, no link with an evil conscience, amen, *an absolute innocence* **that gives us a new kind of confidence**.

I want you to note *"**a true heart**"* is not a heart full of questioning and doubt and resistance and un-belief;

It is *a confident heart.*

It is a heart *full of faith.*

…a heart *"**in full assurance of faith;**"*

…a heart *that is* **sprinkled clean**;

…a heart *"**in full assurance;**"*

…a heart ***that is freed*** *from an evil* *conscience*

…and when the heart is CLEANSED BY FAITH,

…when the heart is CLEANSED,

The body is clean also!

When an evil conscience gets removed, <u>*at the same time*</u> ***evil gets removed from the body also!***

Your body is just a glove, *and the glove only does what the hand tells it to do.*

*Once the heart **gets occupied with and engaged in righteousness and innocence-consciousness** you are free to yield your members **as instruments of that righteousness** and no longer as instruments of sin.*

There is a great difference between *innocence* **and** *ignorance.*

You know, you could enjoy a certain kind of relationship by being ignorant, in today's terms it might be referred to as *tolerance,*

*...*so we just kind of carry on, you know, I couldn't care less what you did in your past, and you couldn't care less what I did in my past, *and what we still might be doing,*

*...*and our ignorance kind of links us together,

But that relationship is very-very shallow and inevitably suspicion begins to build up in that relationship,

*...**and no relationship built upon suspicion can last or be of any real quality.***

The enemy is after the destruction of every relationship. He hates relationship, *and deception is one of the weapons he uses.*

You see, **what is God's ultimate purpose?**

Ephesians 1:10 says that:

10 *"God wants to unite <u>all things</u> IN HIM"*

In other words, God *desires to* **reconcile** <u>everything</u> in Him.

Now that's not just a dream of God. God's not just sitting back and dreaming about this magnificent world *that might be one day,* where everything will be totally *reconciled and united* in Him.

God has planned a redemption in Christ ***that will bring that reconciliation, that unity, about.***

There's truly only one unity that God recognizes.

It's the unity of the Spirit <u>that comes from faith</u>; that comes from the Word of Truth, the gospel of our salvation in Christ.

James 1:18

18 *"Of His own will He brought us forth* (gave us birth, united us to Himself *and one another*) **by the Word of Truth,** *that we might be a kind of first-fruits of His creatures."*

1Corinthians 12:13

13 *"For by one Spirit we were all baptized…"* (In the work of Christ;

…in our understanding and embrace of that work,

*…*we were all baptized into Christ; *immersed in His love; immersed into love itself,* **and, therefore,**)

"*…immersed into one body*"

*"For by one Spirit **we were all immersed into one body** (into reconciliation and unity and embrace and harmony with one another)"*

"…whether Jew or Greek, whether slaves or free"

(…whether denominational or non-denominational, whether black or white, whether rich or poor, working class or upper class, educated or uneducated, religious or non-religious, intelligent or not so intelligent, male or female, grownup, teenager or child)

*"For by one Spirit **we were all immersed into one body,** whether Jew or Greek, whether slaves or free, **and have <u>all</u> been made to drink into one Spirit."***

"We have <u>all</u> been made to drink into one Spirit, *the* **Spirit of God Himself; the Spirit of ultimate TRUTH and LOVE.***"*

You know the enemy so easily traps us in *our endeavor to accomplish unity* that **we forsake The Truth,**

...that **we forsake the foundation that God has given through Truth,**

...that *we try and accomplish a unity **through compromise,** and through,*

'*...well **let's just forget about this issue and overlook that issue**, and let's just ignore this spiritual reality and write off that spiritual reality...*'

But God wants to <u>birth</u> *the kind of unity <u>that is the fruit of the work of redemption</u>,*

...**the work of the blood of Jesus,**

...**not just some hypocritical religious unity,**

...*some politically correct kind of unity,*

...**some <u>second hand kind of unity</u>**

...**that is no** *real* **unity,**

...**no** *real* **unity** *of love*,

...**no <u>real</u> LOVE,**

...**no *<u>real</u> union* at all!**

James 1:21

21 *"Therefore lay aside all filthiness and overflow of wickedness"*

How?

"...receiving with meekness the <u>implanted</u> Word, <u>which is able to save your souls</u>"

I say again:

God wants to birth *the kind of unity, the kind of union that is <u>the fruit</u> of the work of redemption,*

...the work of the blood of Jesus,

<u>...the kind of unity that is based on the Word of Truth</u>

...on *righteousness*, on *acceptance* in Christ,

...the kind of union that is based on *innocence*

...because of *restored identity*,

...not some fake, assumed, false identity;

...some inferior identity inherited in the fall.

The fall of man has been reversed, amen!

It has been cancelled!

Redemption and restoration of our true selves, of our original identity, of the original image and likeness of God we were

made in, which is still in us, <u>happened in Christ</u>!

You see I want us to appreciate *innocence,*

…because I believe that *innocence* is the only key to real relationship; *authentic relationship!*

It is that same relationship of *innocence* that God wants us to begin to live in, in our relationship with one another, *where there is no longer suspicion,* **but the kind of love that seals everything.**

Not because we're trying to just sweep the dirt under the carpet,

…<u>but because we're getting the dirt defeated under the blood,</u>

…and we recognize *the integrity* and *the cleansing power* of the blood of Jesus,

…we recognize *the reality of that complete release* <u>that came to us</u> through the blood of Jesus

…<u>so that we can walk blameless and innocent in the midst</u>…

Can you imagine the crookedness and the perverseness of relationships in the world, *the kind of acceptance that is actually nothing other than denial, choosing to ignore and overlook sin?*

They live empty lives torn apart by suspicion, shame and *separation,* and the shallowness of their relationships are apparent.

That kind of acceptance is actually no acceptance at all, *a loveless acceptance.*

Even if they manage to stay together, they live so far apart.

Now can you imagine how the relationships *of those who embrace the redemptive work of the Lord Jesus Christ* will begin to be the mightiest testimony in the world?

John 13:35

35 *"By **this** they will know that you are My disciples..."*

*"By **this** they will know…"*

*"…they will **know**…"*

'…They will not be able to ignore the brightness, the light that shines forth from your inner-man

*…**because of that innocence that you enjoy in Christ Jesus**,*

*…because of **that life and joy and love radiating out of you,***

...emanating from you ...and <u>from one another</u>,

...as we, <u>together</u>, enjoy one another'

*"By **this** they will **know**..."*

*"...by **the love we have**..."*

*"...by the love we have **for one another**..."*

*"...and also... by the love we have **for them!**"*
(2Corinthians 5:14-21)

Let's get back to our scripture in Hebrews 10;

...so, the Scriptures say here in Hebrews 10:22,

"...that **we can draw NEAR to God,** *no longer with a guilt-consciousness and feeling totally inferior,* **that we can't do it, we can't draw NEAR,**

...but we <u>do</u> draw NEAR,

...<u>with the knowledge that our hearts are cleansed from an evil conscience</u>"

Amen! Praise God!

That's what He desires <u>for every one of us</u>,

...we know that from verse 23.

Hebrews 10:23

23 *"let us then hold fast the confession of our faith without wavering."*

Verse 19 of Hebrews 10 begins with:

"Therefore brethren…"

So that *"therefore,"* would point back to something that is revealed earlier on in the Scriptures.

I mean on what basis can we approach God *with innocence?*

On what basis *can I receive that washing and that cleansing* of a defiled conscience; of a guilty conscience; of a sin-consciousness; of the conscience that I am just a sinful man,

…the Bible calls it *an evil conscience,*

…on what basis can I receive a release from that thing, freedom from it,

…freedom from that *inferior identity,*

…freedom from *that old mentality* of I am just a mere man, a sinner, and evil has rule over me,

…freedom from *guilt and shame and condemnation;*

…<u>a defiled conscience</u>,

…On what basis can I receive that washing and that cleansing; that freedom…?

On the basis of <u>The Truth</u>.

In Christ Jesus, you have been <u>redeemed</u> and <u>restored</u> to your *authentic original design*.

You have been <u>restored</u> to *righteousness* and *true holiness*;

You have been <u>restored</u> to *true innocence!*

You have been <u>released</u>, by the blood of Jesus, *to give full expression to the image and likeness of God,* <u>which is still in you</u>, in which you have been made!

It's on the basis of <u>the blood of Jesus</u>!

In 1John 3:19-22 John says:

19 *"By this we shall know **we are of** The Truth and reassure our hearts before Him"*

20 *"For if our hearts condemn us, **God is greater than our hearts, and knows all things**."*

21 *"Beloved, **if our hearts does not condemn us**, we have confidence towards God."*

22 *"and we receive from Him whatever we ask because we keep* (we believe, we treasure) *His commandments* (the things New Covenant realities instructs us in and persuades us to believe) *and* (therefore) *do what pleases Him…"*

19 *"By this we shall know **we are of The Truth…"***

You see we are not born of some new idea or some philosophy of man. **We are born of God; we come from above;**

Our Daddy came in person, in Jesus Christ, and redeemed us and reconciled us and restored us to our original place in Him…

He released us to live again in our original design, to give full expression again to our true identity as His kids; as His very image and likeness!

*God is Spirit, and because you are a spirit-being, and because God is the Father of all spirits, from whom every family in heaven and on earth is named, **He gave your spirit birth,***

…and doubly, *because He personally came to redeem and rescue and reconcile us to Himself again, and restore us again, **He has the greatest claim upon our lives!***

You are not the product of your parent's desire, and you are not an oops either. **You are not a mistake!**

God desired you!

God skillfully and uniquely formed and fashioned you!

He gave your spirit birth!

He placed you in your mother's womb, *and there He clothed you with flesh* (Psalm 137:l3-14).

You are more than flesh and blood!

You are in all reality your Daddy's offspring!

Made exclusively for Him to love and have a relationship with!

Therefore, He has the greatest claim upon your life!

You see in Christianity we are not dealing with some new idea or some philosophy that another man has thought up, some cleverly devised myth, a new religion that will kind of, you know, promise to man a new relationship filled with innocence, a relationship of bliss with God; a relationship of righteousness…

No! No myth of philosophy or religion can ever give you that!

When we are dealing with **the gospel,** *we are dealing with* **God.**

We are not dealing with religion; ***we are dealing with eternal truth.***

We are dealing with that which was from the beginning, a romance that existed between God and us, *in his heart,* from the very beginning!

We are dealing with God's own revelation of what has been in His heart.

We are dealing with God's self-revelation.

We are dealing with God's own plan of redemption and reconciliation and restoration of man.

We are dealing with love Himself, who came in person, to convince us of His love for us, and our worth and value to Him, and to reveal to us who we truly are, and convince us of it.

He says:

1John 3:19,

19 *"By this* (…by this gospel; by this love; by this work of redemption that God came and

accomplished Himself to reconcile us and to restore us; by THIS) **_we shall know_** *we are of* **_The Truth_**...*"*

That means our experience is of *integrity.*

...**it is born of** *reality,*

...**and** *we have embraced it.*

...**and** ***now our experience of innocence and righteousness is bearing witness to its truth.***

Our experience isn't just a new philosophy that we're holding onto, desperately, <u>to try and overlook and excuse our misconduct</u>, to try and excuse our past,

No!

Our experience of innocence and righteousness is born of *"The Truth."*

1John 3:19

19 *"...and (now because of* **"The Truth"** *that we are God's kids; that we are righteous again; that we are innocent; because of* **"The Truth"** *we can)*

...<u>***reassure our hearts before Him***</u>.*"*

Chapter 4

Reassuring our hearts before God

Do you know that your heart needs to be reassured?

When?

Verse 20 of 1John 3 say:

20 *"...**whenever our hearts condemn us**"*

You see your heart is acutely sensitive, your heart will condemn you, and that condemnation will keep you out of the presence of God

...and you'll begin to feel burdened with guilt and burdened with shame and you think,

'How can I approach God; how can I still draw NEAR to Him, how can I still enjoy closeness, how can I still be that close with Him, I failed Him, I can't do it'

But now the Word says we can *"reassure,"* **in this** *"Truth,"* you can *"reassure your heart."*

In this *"Truth"* of Christ Jesus, in what He <u>fully</u> accomplished, you can *"reassure your heart"*

And now we think,

'But how can we "reassure our hearts?" I mean these are the facts; this actually happened…'

And here we are; we are *cut off* from the presence of God.

Thank God the Scriptures continue to say:

1John 3:20

20 *"…**For God is greater than our hearts**…"*

You see we're facing the highest courts of justice. **It's called the throne of grace.**

The blood of Christ has been applied to the mercy seat. The throne that, in the Fall, used to be the judgment seat, *has now become the mercy seat, **the throne of grace.***

There we are and our hearts accuse us, and the enemy laughs at us, and he points his finger, and the accuser of the brethren is shouting out all kinds of claims against us,

BUT, God says to you:

<u>'I'm greater than the witness of your heart.'</u>

<u>You must see that, in the courts of justice,</u>
<u>God has a greater, more important, more</u>
<u>accurate witness He relies on</u>.

The Bible says in 1John 2:1

1 *"My little children, I am writing this **to you**…"*

…And then John also writes there earlier on about the confessing of our sin *and about the fact that the blood cleanses us from all unrighteousness.*

He says:

*"…**not as an excuse** for sin…"*

But better yet he says:

1John 2:1

1*"…**so you <u>may</u> not sin,**"*

1John 2:1-2

1 *"…**but if** (not when, but <u>**if**</u>) anyone does sin <u>**we have an advocate**</u> before the Father"*

2 *"**who Himself is also the propitiation for our sin,** Jesus Christ the righteous, and **not for ours only but also for the whole world**."*

That advocate, Jesus Christ the righteous, stands in a legal office **on man's behalf**.

That's what the word *"**propitiation**"* stands for:

Jesus was sent by God the Father. He didn't just come on His own, He was sent, …in other words His coming was **legal,**

He was sent to come and accomplish the legal work of redemption on man's behalf,

*"…**not only on our behalf, but on behalf of the whole world***"

…and more than that,

He was raised up and exalted to the right hand of God the Father, to forever uphold and enforce, that legal work of redemption that he accomplished *for us all*.

I say again:

Jesus Christ, the righteous, stands in a legal office on man's behalf.

He holds the legal office of advocate.

That means Jesus occupies a ministry right now *that is legal.*

He's not taking chances before God. *He's not trying to just work a little deal with God* saying:

'O God, you know, this one, he has stumbled again, and you know we've had trouble with

him, but oh let's just give him a chance you know, and just sneak him in.'

No! Jesus operates in a legal office. There's a legal <u>reality</u> behind His ministry, and that reality is found in His blood and His resurrection and His substitutionary work on that cross on our behalf. Amen!?

You see, **<u>you cannot both owe a debt and have the debt paid in full!</u>**

<u>And you see, the Father recognizes that.</u>

<u>That is what makes God greater than our hearts</u>.

The enemy would seek to focus on your heart to bring all kinds of anxieties into your heart to tear you away from the presence of God,

Because as I've said earlier,

...the value of Christianity, the value of what we enjoy with God is found in only one thing.

It's not in how many times we've gone to church, and how many times you've read your Bible, and how many times we've done this or that.

It's found in one thing,

INNOCENCE

It's only found in your personal intimate relationship with God *because of that innocence.*

That's the value of your faith. Amen!?

1John 3:20

20 *"...God is greater than our hearts, **and He knows everything**..."*

And we think,

*'Oh that makes it worse, because you know God knows everything and we can't deny anything or hide anything from Him, He knows **everything**'*

BUT you see, God does not dwell on your ugly old past.

God has better things to occupy His mind with.

The Scriptures says in another place that **He is *ever mindful* <u>of us</u>.**

<u>**God's mind is full of YOU**</u>!

And we think,

'Oh I can't afford that you know, because I don't want God to know all things about my life you know.'

BUT you know what fills Gods' mind?

The <u>reality</u> of the *new creation*.

Gods' mind is filled with the reality of the *new creation*,

...the reality of the New Covenant,

...the reality of your sonship restored!

<u>Gods' mind is filled with the reality of your acceptance in the Beloved;</u>

<u>...of your total redemption and restoration in Him</u>

Gods' mind is filled with the reality of your righteousness and true innocence;

...the reality of your original design;

...the reality of your true identity!

So the Word says:

1John 3:20

20 *"...When our hearts condemn us God is greater than our hearts and He knows everything.*"

He knows the accurate and total implication of Jesus' death on your behalf.

He knows that He was wounded for our transgression and bruised for our iniquities.

Praise God!

1John 3:21

21 *"Beloved, **if our hearts does not condemn us, <u>we have confidence towards God</u>**."*

"Beloved…"

I enjoy John's relationship with the believers.

He's not writing from a point of condemnation.

I mean he could condemn.

Jesus Himself could condemn,

…but Jesus says in John 3:

John 3:17

17 *"I didn't come to condemn, **but I came that the world might be saved through Me**."*

1John 3:21

21 *"**if our hearts does not condemn us, <u>we have confidence towards God</u>**"*

Jeanne Guyon wrote in one of her books:

"It is a good thing to have forgotten your sins ...so that you can remember only God."

You see, sin-consciousness cancels out your son-consciousness;

BUT son-consciousness cancels out both sin-consciousness and sin altogether!

1John 3:21-22

21 *"**if our hearts does not condemn us, <u>we have confidence towards God</u>***"

22 *"and we receive from Him whatever we ask* **because we keep His commandments (we embrace and believe His emphatic truth about us)** *and* **(therefore, as a result, a logical outcome)** *do what pleases Him..."*

Philippians 2:13

13 *"...for* **<u>He</u>** *is at work within us* **<u>both to will and to do</u>** *what pleases Him"*

Why?

Because you see, everything that we live, that we do, *that we are*, relates to and encourages the working of His Spirit within us,

...and we're not apposing; we're not rebelling to the working of His Spirit within us.

So, that confidence we gain *from His truth;*

...from His working within us,

...that makes us who we are,

...now releases us to ask of God,

...and to receive from Him!

Praise the Lord!

Chapter 5

"See what love the Father has given us…"

If you would turn the page with me to 1 John chapter 4

Actually, I want to read verse 28 of chapter 2 first:

1John 2:28

28 *"And now little children, **abide in Him, so that** when He appears **we may have confidence and not shrink from Him in shame** at His coming…"*

Do you see here in this verse that the apostle John challenges us?

John's challenge …actually God's challenge upon the believer is:

To <u>live</u> *enjoying innocence and blamelessness*,

…<u>to actually be</u> without blemish,

…*without reproach*

...in the midst of a crooked and perverse generation

Now if that wasn't possible, then God would expect too much of us.

Then obviously God has missed it. As if He doesn't know our frame. As if He doesn't know where we come from. As if He doesn't know how weak we are. As if He doesn't know our opposition's strength. As if He doesn't know how often we'd like to stumble and fall into misery...

But the truth is, the witness of God is much greater,

That's why He challenges the Church to walk blameless before Him,

...because He has made the kind of provision *to keep us blameless and innocent*,

...without blemish before Him

You see, God didn't just give us righteousness like a cloak you can put on and take off whenever you feel like it;

He didn't just add righteousness to us as part of our ensemble

...He didn't just add righteousness to you;

He made you completely righteous!

You are not just innocent by the blood of Jesus, no, *innocent is who you are!*

You are not just seen as righteous,

...as if God has to deceive Himself when He looks at you,

...as if He has to put on His rose-colored Jesus-glasses when He looks at you,

No, you are not just seen as righteous, *it's the nature of your being!*

What a joy to find out that we are *actually* partakers of a nature that *IS* innocent;

...it was not just made somewhat innocent by the blood of Jesus,

No, *it IS innocent!*

We are partaking of a life that IS righteous and innocent, *and has been from the very beginning!*

That *original life,*

...that *authentic expression* has been restored to us,

...the *very image and likeness* of God,

…our very sonship,

…*our true identity!*

So He says there in 1John 2:28 in other words that,

…if we *"**abide in Him**, (if we abide in the truth about us and Him, in the truth of our true identity as children of God, offspring of God, fully restored to us; if we* **ABIDE** *in intimate fellowship and relationship with Him* **because of the truth;** *in that innocence and righteousness)"*

…then *"at His appearing* **we will not shrink back through shame."**

*"**We may have confidence,**"* He says,

*"…**and not shrink from Him in shame** at His coming."*

You see, that shrinking away from God testifies of *a guilt-consciousness* and *a consciousness of weakness;* that shrinking away from God testifies of *a consciousness of sin, a consciousness of unworthiness* **that keeps us outside of the presence of God.**

Verse 1 of chapter 3:

1 *"**See what love the Father has given us that we should be called children of God**."*

This is so precious and vital for us to see and grasp and treasure and enjoy and rejoice in.

He says:

1 John 3:1

1 *"See what love the Father has given us..."*

He has given us the kind of love *a child can only receive from their parent.*

He says:

1John 3:1

1 *"See what love* (what tremendous love and acceptance) *the Father has given us that we should be called children of God."*

Long before you're a minister, or a pastor, or a worker, **you're His child**.

Praise God for the work of the ministry, *but God wants children in the first place,* not machines that are just doing and working and laboring all the time.

He wants Marys *who know the place at His feet.*

Only Marys make the best Marthas.

He's available to Mary and Martha, *but if we're distracted,* you know, *we can so easily get distracted in our job that we're doing, that we're losing out in sonship,*

…we're losing out on our birthright,

…we're losing out on experiencing and enjoying that love.

…we're losing out on intimacy and eventually on our sense of innocence;

*…our **enjoyment of** innocence and righteousness and intimacy*

1John 3:1-3

1 ***"See what love the Father has given us that we should be called children of God, and so we are**…*

(Not, *'so we might be one day when we're good enough'* or *'so we might be one day when we get to Heaven.'*

No!

*"**SO WE ARE**")*

*"…**The reason why the world does not know us is that it did not know Him.**"*

2 *"Beloved, we are God's children **now** (**N-O-W, NOW**);"*

"…it does not yet appear what we shall be, but **we know that <u>when He appears we shall be like Him</u>,** *for we shall see Him as He is…"*

*"…<u>**we shall be like Him**</u>…"*

We will not be caught up in an inferiority complex when He appears, so that when He appears we look at Him and suddenly we shrink back through shame…

3 *"…and everyone who thus hopes in Him* **purifies himself (in faith and true love from the heart)** *even as He is pure."*

I want you to see a great truth here.

You see, in 1Corinthians 15:52 the Bible speaks about,

52 *"…in the twinkling of an eye …we shall be changed…"*

…and we have misinterpreted that and we thought well in that twinkling of an eye *then God's going to wash away all our sins and all the dirt and all the rubbish and so, quickly, just like that, then He's going to get us ready for Heaven.*

Not so!

He was only speaking about these mortal bodies of ours that will put on immortality in a twinkling of an eye,

He is not speaking about your spirit-man, your inner-man,

Because the Bible says there, back in 1 John 3, that:

1John 3:3,

3 *"...everyone who thus hopes in Him **purifies himself** <u>**even as He is pure**</u>."*

That means I am not trying to get some standard of holiness and start striving for that,

*...but **I purify myself***...

*...**I purify my heart** <u>**through faith**</u>,*

*...**I see His love**,*

*...**I see that He's my Daddy**,*

*...**I see that He has always loved me**,*

*...**I know** <u>**and believe**</u> **the love He has for me**,*

*...**and I fall in love**.*

It happens to me **through faith;**

...as I am embracing His word;

...as He is releasing the working of His power within me,

...which comes to my spirit through the revelation of His Truth,

...and of The Truth of His love.

So when The Truth comes to me,

...when faith comes to me,

I know that <u>I am a child of God</u> <u>NOW</u>! Amen!?

I know that I am loved. Amen!?

I am not praying *towards* redemption, *towards* forgiveness, but I am rejoicing *from* forgiveness, *from* redemption, *from* the position of sonship and being a child of God,

...*from* knowing that I can enjoy innocence, *from* knowing that I am loved and accepted, *from* knowing that *I am* righteous and innocent!

Praise the Lord! Hallelujah!

It is so wonderful to discover that we do not just have a little bit of light in the Lord, no; *we <u>ARE</u> light, in the Lord!*

Chapter 6

"…As He is so are we <u>in this world</u>…"

So let's go now to chapter 4 of 1 John, and we'll start reading from verse 13.

1John 4:13-21

13 **"By this we know that we abide in Him and He in us**,"

"…**because He has given us of His own Spirit (the Spirit of truth)**."

"…**because the love of God, that pours forth from within us, has been awakened in our hearts** by the Holy Spirit (the Spirit of truth; God's own Spirit, exclusively belonging to and proceeding from both the Father and the Son,) **who was given to us**." (Romans 5:5)

14 "And we have seen and testify of the Father that He has sent His Son **as the Savior of the world**"

15 **"Whoever <u>confesses</u> that Jesus is the Son of God, <u>God abides in Him and he in God</u>**."

If we take a look in the Greek at the word HOMOLOGAO which is the word for: *"confesses"* or *"confession"* that is used here,

…we see it is **to be united in the same thought and language**.

That means I am united with God in His opinion;

in His Truth concerning Jesus and concerning what Jesus accomplished for me.

That means I am united with God in His opinion;

in His Truth concerning me.

I no longer see myself as a fallen man,

…**but as a redeemed man,**

I see myself as a new creature,

…**and because of that, my confession is that,**

I know Jesus to be the Son of God, my Savior.

He has delivered me from the power of darkness, and translated me into the Kingdom of His Father,

...into the glorious liberty of the sons of God!

It goes on to say here in 1John 4:16,

16 *"...**And so we know, and so we have believed** (and actually actively still believe) the love God has for us."*

*"...**God is love, and he who abides in that love** (in the love God has for us) abides in God, and God abides in him."*

17 *"In this...* (In this knowledge you see, because we know, **and we believe**)*"*

*"...**In this** believing is love **perfected in us**..."*

Then he goes on to say, this is:

*"... **in order that we may have confidence** in the day of judgment..."*

1John 4:17

17 *"...**we may have confidence** in the day of judgment*

(*...*or whenever an accusation comes against us; whenever the accuser of the brethren starts with His attacks and his lies and deception *...*we have confidence in that day,)

*...**because as He is, so are we**, in this world,*

(…we know who our true Daddy is, and we know we are our Daddy's kids!)"

"…***as He is, so are we***…"

"…***As much as he is in love with us, so are we, we are in love with Him also***."

We reflect, we emanate, and represent Him in this world,

…His love for us,

…His nature,

…His very character,

…who He truly is!

We are the offspring of His love, produced, and brought forth by Him, in His love.

We are the product of who He is, *of His love for us*.

We are His image, His likeness;

…we are reflecting, we are emanating and exhibiting that,

…we are representing Him as His own dear children

"…***as He is, so are we, in this world***…"

John 1:12 says,

12 *"...But as many as received Him, to them He gave the right to become (he gave us the ability and permission, through revelation into The Truth,) to feel like and behave like..."*

Literally it says:

"He restored to us the power to be; He gave us the legal right to be, beloved children of God, even to those who believe in His name..."

(To those who believe in His reputation, in who He is; in His character, in His integrity; the integrity of what he has done for us in redemption; the integrity of His love.)

The Mirror Translation actually gives us the best interpretation according to the original Greek of what is being said and meant in John 1:12:

"Everyone who realizes their association in Him, convinced that He is their original life and that His name defines them, in them He endorses the fact that they are indeed His offspring, begotten of Him; He sanctions the legitimacy of their sonship."

(The word often translated, "to receive," LAMBANO, means to comprehend, grasp, to identify with. This word suggests that even

though He came to His own, there are those who do not grasp their true origin revealed in Him, and like the many Pharisees they behave like children of a foreign father, the father of lies [John 8:48].

Neither God's legitimate fatherhood of man nor His ownership is in question; man's indifference to his true origin is the problem. This is what the Gospel addresses with utmost clarity in the person of Jesus Christ. Jesus has come to introduce man to himself again; humanity has forgotten what manner of man he is; his design! [James 1:24; Deut 32:18; Ps 22:27].

The word, GENESTHAI [aorist tense], is like a snapshot taken of an event, from GINOMAI, to become [See John 1:3]. The LOGOS is the source; everything commences in Him. He remains the exclusive Parent reference to their genesis. There is nothing original, except the Word! Man began in God [See also Acts 17:28]. "He came to give us understanding, to know Him who is true, and to realize that we are in Him who is true" [1John 5:20].

The word, EXOUSIA, often translated "power;" as in, He gave "power" to become children of God, is a compound word; EK, always denoting origin or source and EIMI, I am; thus, out of I am! This gives legitimacy and authority to our sonship; TEKNON, translated as offspring, child.

*"He has given," DIDOMI, in this case to give something to someone that already belongs to them; thus, to return. The fact that they already are His own, born from above, they have their beginning and their being in Him **is now confirmed in their realizing it!**
Convinced, PISTEO; His name ONOMA, defines Man [See Eph 3:15]. "He made to be their true selves, their child-of-God selves." – The Message Bible)* – This whole passage about John 1:12 was taken from *THE MIRROR BIBLE* Copyright © 2012, by Francois du Toit.

Our confidence in perhaps some future Day of Judgment is based on the Day of Judgment that took place already when God judged sin; *when God already judged us in His Son*

...it is not built on a vain hope that perhaps, you know, God will excuse us because we've tried so hard you know,

...because we've gone to church so often, and we've prayed so much, and we've fasted, and we've cried, and we've tried our best

No!

Our confidence has a stronger foundation than our good works or our trying to be good.

Our confidence is based on the successful work of redemption!

Our confidence is in the God who is greater than our hearts,

...in the God who knows everything,

...who knows the integrity of the Blood Covenant.

So, my confidence is in that,

...so I need not shrink back at His appearing and fear that there will be some other, yet another future Day of Judgment and rejection, and separation and death for me.

Why not?

Because,

"...**_As He is so are we_**..."

Because,

"...**_we_** (intimately) **_know and have believed the Love He has for us_**"

Because,

"(His) *perfect love* (for us) **_casts out all fear_**"

Because,

"(as a result of THAT perfect love **He has for us**) ...*purifies himself* **_even as He is pure_**."

96

When Jesus said in John chapter 14:

John 14:3,

3 *"...I go to prepare a place for you ...**so you may be where I am**"*

He was speaking about His cross, His death on the cross. He was speaking about the fruit of the Judgment Day that took place in Him.

Some translations use the word *"mansion"* earlier on there in verse 2 and has given us the idea that God's building a fabulous mansion in Heaven for us, but in fact, that word, *"mansion"* is the same word that is used in John 15, where Jesus speaks about,

John 15:4,

4 *"...**abiding** in Me as the branch **abides** in the vine"*

It speaks of *an abode, a dwelling place*.

Not a shadow, off in the future, but *the substance now,* an *intimate relationship* with God now.

He says:

John 14:3,

3 *"...**so that you may be where I am**..."*

And He says in John 14,

John 14:10,

10 *"...I am in my Father and my Father is in Me"*

There's no distance between Jesus and the Father.

There's no suspicion.

...there is no unresolved and unsettled judgment between them,

...there's absolute innocence.

In fact, John 1:18 says,

18 *"The Son, **who is in the bosom of the Father**, He has revealed Him."*

And now He says, John 14:3

3 *"...and **I go to prepare a place** (an equal place; that place; that same place) **for you**."*

That's my place, hallelujah!

That's the only place I desire in God.

It's a place *to be "**as He is**,"*

*...of being "**as He is**."*

That place speaks of that *absolute innocence* and the *absolute satisfaction* that is *enjoyed* in the relationship between the Father and His Son.

Such oneness, to where the Son gives full expression to the Father, because He dwells in that full embrace.

One heart, one mind, one conversation, one expression!

1John 4:17,

17 "**We have confidence** for the Day of Judgment, **because as He is, so are we**, in this world."

Verse 18 says:

1John 4:18,

18 "**There is no fear in love**, but **perfect love casts out fear**...

How is love perfected?

If you read just a little earlier on it will tell you:

1John 4:16

16 "In **this**..."

In what?

In *"this **faith**"*

... in *"**this** experience"*

... in *"**this** place we abide in and enjoy"*

... in that <u>**we believe and know the love God has for us**</u>.

*In **that**, in **this place**, is love perfected, and in **this place** is fear cast out!*

*In **this place**, of **understanding**, and **believing**, and **knowing**!*

That means, I identify myself with the love God has for me,

I believe it, and I know it,

...and *through that identification* I realize and find myself, that, as He is, so am I, in this world;

...in love with Him, as He is in love with me,

...purifying myself, even as He is pure.

I identify myself with the love God has for me.

...and *through that identification* I realize and find myself to be His child, His offspring, His image and likeness in the midst of a crooked and perverse generation,

...I find myself, identifying myself, and associating myself with Him, as His child, as His bride.

...as He is, so am I, in this world!

And what happens?

That perfect love, *that is now perfected in me,* casts out fear.

What fear is He talking about?

Fear that has to do with some future punishment,

...or punishment of any other kind!

Chapter 7

"...Now no condemnation..."

1John 4:18

18 *"There is no fear in love,"*

*"...but **perfect love casts out fear**,"*

*"...**for fear has to do with punishment**."*

That's why I don't need to shrink back from Him at His coming.

That's why I don't need to fear and be anxious about,

'Perhaps I'm not going to be good enough when Jesus appears,'

...because I know that, **that perfect love,** that is perfected **in** me,

...not just as a definition outside of me, not just as a Bible doctrine *"that God so loved the world that He gave His only begotten Son,"*

...**but as the working of God within me,**

...that love, that *'agape'* that is fully awakened in my heart, **that now operates within me, the release from a sin-consciousness and a judgment-consciousness, and from sin itself,**

*...***so that with confidence I may now draw NEAR,**

*...*so that, should my heart condemn me...

You see, Paul writes about that in Romans, when he cries out in chapter 7.

He says in verse 1, (and I'm giving just the gist of his heart revealed in Romans 7):

Romans 7:1-25

1 *"...I am writing this **to those who know the law**,"*

'...you've tried to attain to a certain level of righteousness through the law,' he says,

"but you know very well as I have known*...***"**

*'listen, I was a student of the law, I knew the law, I knew what it was like to bluff people, to fool people; I knew what it was to live a life that is blameless according to the law, **on the outside,***' he says,

"...but the very things that I knew was right according to the law, I found myself transgress

*again and again, because of **a stronger force within me,**"*

He says,

"I was addicted because of my desperate inner need. *I was addicted, because I was empty, I was **enslaved** to sin, I was **enslaved** to a power that kept me in bondage."*

In verse 24 he says,

*"Who will deliver me from this body of death...**Is there deliverance from this body of death?***

 He says,

"Is this all there is to religion?"

He says,

"I've given everything I've got for religion, but I'm still empty."*

...**But you see Paul began to witness, in the very group that he was persecuting,** *the evidence of what he was after himself.*

He witnessed it in the face of that young man, Stephen, whose face shone like an angel while he was being stoned,

...**He, witnessed** *an innocence,*

...**no fear of dearth,**

...**no fear of judgment.**

...**he witnessed** *tranquility,*

...*a transparency,* **in that young man,**

... *righteousness!*

He began to doubt his own faith in the law.

And when God challenged him on that road to Damascus, God said to him,

Acts 9:5

5 *"...It's hard for you to kick against the pricks..."*

You see there was a conviction that was working in Paul's spirit, *and he was trying to reject it,*

...because he knew only one way, the way of righteousness through the law, *but he knew it miserably failed him,* because he says there in Romans 7,

Romans 7:15,

15 *"The good things that I know I should do, I do not find how to do it,"*

He says,

*"In my inner man, I agree that the law is good, **but I do not find** how to do it,"*

He says, verse 24:

*"Wretched man that I am, **who will deliver me** from this body of death?"*

He says,

Romans 7:25

25 *"I thank God, through Jesus Christ **there is deliverance** from this law of sin and death."*

And **then** he continues on in Romans 8:

Romans 8:1

1 *"There is **therefore**, **now**, **no condemnation** for those who are in Christ Jesus…"*

*"…**no condemnation**…"*

We don't preach Romans 8:1 as another excuse for sin.

We don't preach 1John 1:9 *"…If we confess our sins He is faithful to forgive us our sins…"* **as an excuse for sin.**

We don't preach Romans 5, the second last verse there, verse 20 *"…where sin increased, grace abounded all the more…"* **as an excuse for sin.**

Because Paul says:

Romans 6:1

1 *"Shall we now remain in sin, so that grace may abound?*

In other words,

"...Shall we take advantage of God's love, shall we take God's love for granted, shall we make light of the blood, shall we make light of that Judgment that already took place, shall we despise it and walk all over it, shall we ignore the successful work of redemption?"

He says,

Romans 6:2

2 *"**By no means**! How can we continue in sin if we died to it?"*

Amen!?

So, that's not my argument; in writing this book;

I don't make any excuse for sin,

I don't argue on behalf of sin,

...**but the reality of this truth is** that,

Romans 8:1

1 *"There **is** now **no** condemnation."*

It is downright strange, demonically strange, how the Church has been fighting for condemnation; *how the Church has been fighting for the right to be sinners.*

You know,

'We're poor miserable old sinners, and so we'll stay, none of us will ever be totally free, we'll just be sinners,'

…and we've been fighting for that right,

Why?

Because we've been trying to justify and accommodate *our own pet sins*

Listen, the New Testament reveals an integrity that legally justifies man;

…that *totally* justifies man,

…and in that we find our source that leads to freedom.

He says that the just requirement of the law is fulfilled.

Judgment already happened.

<u>Justice was satisfied in the sacrifice of Jesus</u>.

You see **that's what's behind my confidence now**.

My confidence is no longer built upon the merit of my own performance,

…thinking,

'Well, you know, at least this week, you know, I've prayed every day, or almost every day, and I've read, you know, so many scriptures, and…

… and I'm trying to base my confidence upon the merit of yesterday's performance, you know*…*

'At least I've been to church twice today, so really, you know, now I can truly face God with a new confidence.'

Listen, **there's a stronger foundation,**

*…***there's a STRONGER foundation to our innocence and our confidence.**

That confidence, that innocence has roots,

*…***it is rooted in the New Covenant.**

Amen!?

And that love **casts out all fear,**

…the fear that has to do with punishment,

…the fear that will cause you to shrink back from the presence of God.

Adam and Eve feared greatly, because of sin, because guilt covered and smothered them.

They couldn't face God, but listen…

1John 4:18,

18 *"…perfect love* **casts out** *all fear…"*

What is that perfect love?

It's the knowledge, *and the faith,* **in** the love that God has for us.

You see, 1John 4:19,

19 *"…**He first loved us**…"*

19 *"**We love Him, because He fist loved us**"*

Romans 5:8,

8 *"…**God demonstrates His own love towards us, in that,** while we were still sinners, **Christ died for us** (and took our Judgment upon Himself)"*

Chapter 8

Innocence is Bliss

I often use this illustration in counseling people,

I would say that perhaps the two of us,

let's take my friend Joel Vause and me as an example;

Joel and I, perhaps we've been great friends in the past, say 10 years ago, you know, we've been devoted friends, we've just genuinely appreciated one another, we've spent much time together, we've often gone on holiday together,

...and then, one day I was in trouble, and I borrowed money from Joel, and I asked him, I said *'Joel, listen, I really, I need hmm…'*

...and Joel was expecting me to say $100.00, and I said, *'$10,000.00…'*

I said, *'listen man, I need $10,000.00 can you help me?'*

And because Joel loves me he helps me.

But try as I may, it seemed as if life itself just turned against me and I could never pay that $10,000.00 back, and so, do you know what came into our relationship?

A tension, strain, came into our relationship;

…it's called guilt,

…it's called sin-consciousness,

…because I can no longer with confidence visit my friend, you see, my excuses that once sounded so good and could ease the tension have grown stale, even in my own mouth.

You see, when I see Joel, I no longer see the marvelous times that we've enjoyed together, I no longer see the nice guy that he is, and the great times that we've had, but I see that $10,000.00, and I feel guilty towards him.

When Joel sees me, he no longer sees me for the friend I use to be, but there's a resentment that challenges his love in his heart, there's resentment, and he feels ugly towards me because of that money.

You see, there's a guilt now that has risen between us and separated us in our friendship.

Now I cannot approach Joel. He's got to take the initiative.

You see he has to consider in his own mind that our friendship is worth more to him than that $10,000.00.

In fact, it was more than $10,000.00, it was millions, you see, because...

Matthew 16:26,

26 *"what shall man give to redeem his soul?"* *"What is the price of a man's soul?"*

That separation is complete.

But, God so loved the world, He first loved us, He loved us while we were still sinners, and He removed Judgment out of the equation, He took our Judgment upon Himself.

You see **we need to know the love of God and believe that love**.

It's not just a knowledge in principle, a dogmatic knowledge. You know: *"The Doctrine Of The Love Of God,"*

...but **it's the believing, the appropriating of that love,**

...***knowing* that** *God no longer counts my trespasses against me.*

I'm now free to agree with God.

I'm agreeing with <u>God</u>!

You see, Joel could approach me, or he could write his own little Bible, his own little legal document, he could write a little letter and say,

'Rudi, I've considered this thing, and I've decided to pay that debt myself because I love you.'

He says,

'Now Rudi, I want you to forget about that debt, let go of your guilt and let's enjoy fellowship again.'

You see, before Joel could take that step, he had to calculate in his own mind, he had to get the memory in his own mind sorted out, because had he approached me, and every time he sees me, and hears my voice, perhaps yet another apology, yet another excuse, that memory would again revive, it will again bring back the same situation.

And now also, if I believed Joel, and I approach him, and all the time I'm so conscious of my own failure, and every five minutes I remind him, I say,

'O Joel, I'm so sorry man, I seriously dropped you, and treated you wrong, and you know…'

What will happen?

I'll tell you what will happen,

…it will again cause the same strain in the relationship.

Joel doesn't delight in that.

Joel doesn't now feel,

'Well, now I'm superior to you, because, you know, you failed me, and I have forgiven you, and now you better just stay on your side of the line you know. I'll call you when I need you; Don't call me, I'll call you when I want to.'

You see that will be no reconciliation,

…**there'd be no restoration,**

It'll be a false thing.

Joel wants a totally restored relationship, restored as it used to be and even better, yes **BETTER!**

Hallelujah!

You see if the New Covenant could not introduce me to a new relationship with God that is equal, or even better, than what Adam enjoyed in the garden, *then the New Covenant has failed!* I'm telling you.

And religion never saw this truth.

If I cannot be restored to an equally, innocent, walk with God, as what Adam enjoyed before the fall, then the New Covenant has failed, then it's just another failure.

Now I believe, that when God says,

Hebrews 10:17,

17 *"I will remember your sins **no more**,"*

God means business.

I believe that!

I believe that God takes no delight *in calculating our trespasses* you see.

I believe that there's no pleasure in the heart of God, *to think about our past*.

This is why He says,

2Corinthians 5:17,

17 *"Therefore, If any man is in Christ, he's a new creation; **the old things have passed away**, behold **everything** has become new."*

And that newness has a foundation to it,

…it's not a dream; *it's a reality,*

Amen!?

118

This is then why Paul says,

Philippians 3:13,

13 *"...One thing I do, <u>forgetting those things</u> <u>which lie behind</u>,"*

He says in other words,

"I'm no longer sitting there and feeling sorry for myself, for my past mistakes,"

He says,

"...I forget those things..."

And he can legally do that, *because God did it*.

He can now *"reckon"* himself dead,

2Corinthians 5:14

14 *"...If One died for all, <u>then all died</u>..."*

He can now *"reckon"* himself alive,

Romans 6:11

11 *"...reckon yourselves to be dead indeed to sin, BUT RATHER, <u>alive to God in Christ Jesus our Lord</u>."*

You see he can now, *"reckon"* himself, **in agreement with God...**

<u>He and God can now enter into a new partnership, into a new relationship</u>.

The prodigal son was not met by a suspicious father,

...was not met by a father who said,

'Yes, but... you know, what about this, that, and the other thing.'

No, *his father completely, totally, obliterated his past,* and invited him into a new relationship, *into a new transparent relationship,*

...no hindrances there, no hidden anything.

That's what God desires, nothing less than that, Amen!?

So, <u>the love that is perfected within us, is the love that originated in the heart of God</u>.

And we just become recipients of that love.

We say,

'God, I want my life to now reflect and exhibit the integrity of your love.'

You see if my heart reflects and exhibits suspicion, **then I'm questioning God's integrity,**

…then I'm saying to Him,

'God I don't think you've, you know, died enough, maybe Jesus need to die again. The price that you paid is inferior, I mean, I'm the worst, I'm downright terrible, I still deserve Judgment… I know you Judged your Son, but I still deserve some… and maybe, secretly, <u>You also, DO feel, just like I do</u>…'

…but instead, now I'm saying,

'God, I recognize the integrity of your plan of salvation. I recognize that that love, totally dealt with the judgment I deserve, and it totally, totally restores me in <u>complete</u> fellowship with You.'

And you see, <u>God reckons that kind of faith and agreement as righteousness</u>.

God is prepared to bear witness along with that truth.

So, 1John 4:18

18 *"…fear has to do with punishment, **and <u>he who fears is not perfected in love</u>**.*"

19 ***"We love Him, <u>because He first loved us</u>***."

Now that's Truth.

What I'm sharing with you in this book **is New Testament Truth,**

...and when you grasp this Truth, *it will liberate you*.

You will never ever again struggle with sin or a sin-consciousness,

...because you'll discover that the power of sin is broken.

It can no longer dominate you.

Romans 6:12

12 *"Let not sin **therefore** rule in your mortal bodies to make you obey its passions,"*

'I'm not going to let that thing boss me around anymore,'

...because there's a new lordship that I recognize in my life,

...it's the lordship of His love,

...it's the lordship of my total fulfillment in Him,

...it's the lordship of His Truth,

...it's the lordship of His life,

...it's the lordship of the Spirit of life in Christ Jesus.

That lordship now liberates me.

But how does it affect our relationship with the brethren?

Let's continue to read:

1John 4:20

20 *"If anyone says, 'I love God,' and yet hates his brother, he's a liar; for he who does not love his brother whom he has seen, cannot love God whom he has not seen."*

21 *"and this commandment we have from Him: that he who loves God should* (as a result) *love his brother also."*

You see, you cannot enjoy the presence of God, *just there in the privacy of your closet,*

…and think,

*'**Well, me and God, we'll have our thing, never mind the rest**.'*

Remember what Jesus said in Matthew 18?

He says,

Matthew 18:35

35 *"Everyone, who does not forgive his brother from his heart, will be tormented…"*

*...*Because what you're actually doing is, *you're canceling the integrity of God's forgiveness*.

Now I don't want to be saying this in a negative sounding way, I want to say it in a positive way,

I want to encourage you to begin to take the new creation reality that relates to your innocence in the presence of God, *and I want you to begin to allow that working to begin to effect your every relationship* on planet earth,

...your <u>every</u> relationship.

<u>Allow the new creation to become the factor of your relationships</u>.

It will introduce a new strength in your marriage, *in your every relationship*.

...it will introduce a new *innocence* that will cause you to be a conqueror.

You will no longer need to be trapped in the lie of having to perform all the time because people like your performance, but you'll be released from the fear of man's opinion, from living for the praise of man.

...you'll be released to walk in the confidence that you walk in in transparency before God.

God will see to it that the favor that you enjoy in relationship with others *will be the result of your innocence in His Word,*

*...*not your performance.

Never mind if they're suspicious,

...never mind if they come with suspicions and arguments,

You just walk *in the fruit of this confidence, in the fruit of this bliss and innocence, in the fruit of this revelation, in the fruit of this love,*

...**and you'll see how your love will become *so attractive* that people will be drawn to you *because of that love,***

...**they'll be drawn to you!**

Because, what's going to happen if this light shines in the midst of a crooked and perverse world?

That crooked world, that perverse world, is going to want to make their crooked ways straight.

Listen, they desire a straight life, they have had enough of that crookedness, they've had enough of that misery and heartache.

They want what we have.

They <u>want</u> what we have.

<u>Because what we have</u> *is legal*.

That means, <u>it's vital for today</u>!

It means, <u>it's real</u>.

Chapter 9

"…no longer any consciousness of sin…"

What we have is not a dream, it's not a philosophy, it's not a religion, ***it's an innocence that is of God,***

…it is a Truth *that is greater than any condemnation.* It is a Truth that is greater than any finger that points against us, and it's a Truth *that sets us free,* and *we remain free* even when fingers of accusation are pointed at us!

Romans 8:33-34

33 ***"Who shall lay <u>any</u> charge against God's elect, <u>if</u> (since) *it is God* (Himself) <u>who justifies</u>?"***

34 ***"<u>Who shall condemn us,</u> if (since) *it is Christ Himself who died, and is risen, and is even now at the right hand of God, making intercession for us?"***

Hey, that's revelation that speaks.

God is involved in my inner-man, in my transformation, __engaging my mind and my spirit, engaging my heart__, *opening my eyes to what He did for me and with me in redemption;*

…relocating me mentally with that truth,

…thus, making me righteous, blameless, spotless, innocent,

…and no devil, not even Satan himself, *can accuse me.*

35 *"…And __nothing__ can separate me from His love,"*

Nothing can separate me from that love,

…that love that is perfected within me by His working within me.

__It casts out__ *all fear, all suspicion, all anxiety, all inferiorities,*

*…*CAST OUT,

…and I'm restored in an innocent, blameless, relationship with God.

That is *the integrity* of the New Covenant.

This message is what the New Testament preaches.

The New Testament does not preach a message of condemnation.

It does not preach and promote a message of man's failure and God's anger towards man.

That's the Old Covenant.

The New Covenant introduces a God who is pleased with the sacrifice of His Son,

...who entered once and for all into the most holy place,

...not taking with Him the blood of bulls and goats,

...but the blood of His own body, which He sacrificed on our behalf, to release us from our sins

He says that that blood cleanses us *from an evil conscience.*

The author of the book of Hebrews *made it obvious* that the tabernacle, and the different arrangements made concerning it under the Old Covenant *was merely a prophetic symbolic picture of the true tabernacle,* preserved in the heavenly realm, speaking not merely about Heaven, but *actually* speaking about our inner-man... *because **we are** the real tabernacle of God.*

Therefore, in speaking about those old prophetic symbolic pictures of the tabernacle, and the different arrangements made concerning it under to the Old Covenant, the author of the book of Hebrews says, that under that Old System:

Hebrews 9:9

9 *"...gifts and sacrifices are offered,* **which cannot perfect the conscience of the worshiper.**"

Let me ask you, why would these things be written in the New Testament?

I mean, if the New Testament was a failure, *if the New Testament could also not perfect the conscience of the worshiper,*

...**then why bother to compare one failure with another?**

You see, and in the way that religion has proclaimed the New Testament, they've proclaimed it as a failure.

They've said to man,

'Well, we're all sinners, you know, even the preacher is a sinner, so we might as well just... I mean, the best we can do is to try our best, and count on God's grace to cover the rest, to cover our weaknesses, really to cover our pet sins we're not willing to let go of.'

That's no gospel! That's a lie! It's deception!

I mean if the Old Covenant *could not perfect the conscience of the worshiper,*

…and the New Testament *also could not perfect the conscience of the worshiper,* then where is the worshiper;

What are we left with?

We are left with nothing; we are left with stale old boring and toxic man made religion that slowly kills us;

…*we are still outside of the presence of God.*

Because our guilt will keep us there!

…**their guilt will keep them there!**

I want you to take your Bible and thickly underline that statement in Hebrews 9,

Hebrews 9:9

9 *"…gifts and sacrifices are offered,* **which cannot perfect the conscience of the worshiper,***"*

Because that's the issue here,

*"…**the conscience of the worshiper**…"*

That's the issue of the New Covenant, it's the *"conscience,"* it's the *"inner man,"*

…**because you cannot experience innocence through ignorance**.

See, what's the use of being innocent, by just trying not to think of all your bad things?

You need something stronger than that.

I mean, you know, if I have cancer in my body, and I just try to ignore the symptoms, and I just say,

'Well, I don't have cancer, I don't have cancer, I don't have cancer,'

'I'm just going to try and keep ignoring it,'

Hey listen, ignoring it is not going to remove it.

You see what I'm saying?

I could act like I don't have it, but that thing is ultimately going to kill me if I just try and ignore it.

Same thing with sin!

See, this message isn't just,

'Ah, let's just ignore our failure and our sins,'

132

But, it's actually, literally, taking that ugly thing, that law of sin and death *and confronting it face to face with the gospel of Jesus Christ,*

...and <u>allowing the Spirit *through the Word, through Truth* to deal with that thing</u>

...*and destroying that demonic stronghold in your thinking and in your spirit, in your inner-man.* **Amen!?**

Alright, Hebrews 9:9

9 *"...gifts and sacrifices are offered, which cannot perfect **the conscience of the worshiper**,*

Verse 10 says,

10 *"but it deals only with food and drink and various washings and baptisms, <u>**regulations for the body**</u> (only)...* **(It doesn't even come close to touching the inner-man)**

10 *"...**imposed** <u>**until**</u> the time of reformation,"*

10 *"...imposed until **<u>the time of</u>** reformation,"*

And I'm telling you now, **that time has come, the fullness of time has already come; that reformation has already come, in the incarnation, in Jesus Christ, in the work of redemption.**

It's not a prophetic thing that we're speaking about like Paul in 1Thessalonians 4:13-18 and 1Corinthians 15:20-28.

(He was speaking prophetically about **the transforming of our bodies only**, when mortality will put on immortality in the resurrection, in the coming again of Christ. **He was not speaking about our spirits. He was not speaking about the transforming of our inner-man, only the transforming of our bodies**.)

Hebrews 9:11

11 *"...but when Christ appear**ed** (**past tense***), *as a High Priest of the good things **having come about***"

(The Greek actually, literally, says *"**having come about**"*)

...You see, some translators didn't grasp this revelation, so they still put it out in the future tense as something that might be, maybe one day, maybe in Heaven someday, but I'm glad that the Revised Standard Version got it right when they wrote it this way,

11 *"...**of the good things <u>that have come</u>**,"*

Because the gospel is a present tense reality, it's happened, it's not going to happen, <u>it's happened</u>, Amen!?

Hebrews 9:12

12 *"...Then, through the greater and more perfect tent, not made with hands, that is, not of this creation,* **He entered <u>once</u> and for <u>all</u>** *into the holy place,"*

13 *"not taking the blood of goats and calves, but His own blood,* **thus <u>securing</u> an <u>eternal</u> redemption..."**

I like that wording there:

13 *"...***<u>thus He secured</u> an eternal redemption***"*

The work of Jesus, through His own blood, <u>secures and guarantees</u> my redemption, you see.

My redemption is a <u>guaranteed</u> redemption.

<u>It's the real thing</u>.

It's not a religious substitute.

<u>It's the real thing</u>,

He guarantees it.

He secures <u>an eternal work</u>,

...not just a two week thing, you know, not just for a month, it will last while the goosebumps last kind of thing,

...**but it's an <u>eternal</u> work,**

...**it's an <u>eternal</u> salvation,**

...**it's an <u>eternal</u> covenant.**

God forever redeemed man and forever reconciled man with Himself, in this Gospel.

Then he reflects back to the past again in verse 13

Hebrews 9:13

13 *"...For if the sprinkling of the defiled persons with the blood of goats and bulls, and with the ashes of a heifer, **sanctifies for the purification of the flesh only**..."*

Remember the different ablutions, all those ablutions...

What was their significance?

They were prophetic, all those baptisms, **they were prophetic,**

...because man would, in his washing, he would indicate,

'God I want to remove, as I'm removing dirt from my body, I would want to remove all sin from me, I would want to remove this guilt, I would want to remove this feeling of inferiority,

136

…I want to be able to approach you God, I want to be able to know you intimately, to know you as a friend, to enjoy innocence in your presence again God,

…so with different washings and different regulations I would again approach you, oh God,

…I would again approach you with the blood of bulls and goats and the ashes of a heifer, and I'm trying to purify myself,'

Prophetically it spoke about what was coming about in Christ.

Verse 14 says now,

Hebrews 9:14,

14 *"…**how much more**…"*

Do you see that comparison?

14 *"…**how much more <u>shall</u>** (not maybe, but "**shall**") **the blood of Christ**, who through the eternal spirit, offered Himself **without blemish** to God, <u>**purify our conscience**</u>…"*

Man's religious efforts, the blood of bulls and goats couldn't *touch man's conscience,* your own works, your own sacrifices, <u>no matter how good they are</u>, *couldn't touch your conscience.*

Do you know why?

Because chapter 10:3 says,

Hebrews 10:3

3 *"...in these sacrifices there's a reminder,* **there's a reminder _of sin_**, *year after year..."*

*"...**a reminder _of sin_**..."*

In other words,

*"... **a reminder of,** you failed Me again, you failed Me again, you failed Me again..."*

...and the conscience stays tormented with the memory of its failure,

But verse 14 of chapter 9,

14 *"...**how much more _shall_** ...**the blood of Jesus** ...**purify your conscience** from dead works to serve the living God."*

Praise the Lord forever!

So, chapter 10:1 says,

1 *"...but since the law **is but a shadow** of the good things to come (or "**that has now come,**") **and not the true form of THESE REALITIES**...*

The whole concept of the New Testament, the whole revelation of the New Testament, consist of *"**these realities**."*

*"**These realities**,"* **new creation realities, are the theme of the New Testament.**

E W Kenyon wrote a book called:

THE BIBLE IN THE LIGHT OF YOUR REDEMPTION,

…and I believe it is the only way that you could study the Bible.

If you try and study the Bible, just **from a historical point of view,** you'll get confused.

If you try and study the Bible, just **from a cultural and religious point of view,** you'll get even more confused.

But if you begin to study the Bible **in the light, in the revelation of <u>your</u> redemption,** it's an entirely different story; it's a new book.

Suddenly it's no longer a drag to read the Scriptures; suddenly it's no longer something religious that I've got to force myself to do, but it becomes the most exciting activity of my life, **because I've discovered it's the legal inheritance that God has invested on my behalf**.

This Holy Bible is a legal sacred contract that God introduce to man through the blood of Jesus.

And now I begin to study this Holy Bible in the light of *"**these realities**,"* **not these shadows, but the substance,** *"**these realities**."*

It says in Hebrews 10:1

1*"...**the law is just a shadow**, but we're dealing with the good things **that have come about**... with **these realities** that have come about..."*

*"...so the law can never by these same sacrifices which are continually offered, year after year, **make perfect** (in conscience, in approach, in innocence) those who draw **near**..."*

Why?

2 *"**otherwise**..."*

(Now I want you to notice He is using such logical reasoning here)

2 *"**otherwise**..."*

I mean if they could,

Verse 1,

*"...**make perfect those who draw near**..."*

140

Verse 2 says,

2 *"...**would they not have ceased to be offered**?"*

Because,

Hebrews 10:2

2 *"...If the worshipers **had ONCE been** cleans**ed, they would no longer have any consciousness of sin**..."*

*"If the worshipers **had ONCE been** cleans**ed**..."*

I mean, **if that system was complete,**

...what would be the evidence of it?

NO SIN-CONSCIOUSNESS,

...innocence,

...absolute restored innocence!

Hebrews 10:2

2 *"...**they would no longer have any consciousness of sin**..."*

Listen, I'm telling you now,

...that dispensation of innocence Adam and Eve enjoyed

...is restored through the New Covenant God made

...in fact, God went even further; *the very innocence Jesus Christ Himself enjoys* has been made our portion in the New Covenant

...and is now revealed to man through the gospel.

When the Bible speaks of:

Hebrews 9:10

10 *"...the reformation..."*

In other words,

Acts 3:21

"...the restoration of all things,"

It begins here:

It's a restored fellowship between man and God.

That restoration extends through to our relationships with one another.

That relationship,

...that restored fellowship between us and God breaks down the dividing wall of hostility.

142

…it breaks down every barrier.

Listen, we are no longer praying towards unity,

…the songs we sing, we need to change some of the wording, we no longer need to pray *'Lord make us one,'* **we're beginning to pray from a new oneness.**

We're not working towards oneness, but now,

…we're operating from the revelation of being united with Christ Jesus and one another.

You see that's the revelation of the New Testament,

…it's no longer the shadow, it's the substance.

I'm no longer praying towards healing… *I can die praying for healing, and many have.*

I'm no longer praying for healing,

I'm recognizing that *healing legally belongs to me,* and *I believe* I'm healed, and *I confess it,* and I *lay hold* of it.

Amen!?

I'm recognizing that,

*"…by His stripes I **was** healed."* Amen!?

*"I **was** healed."*

It's a done deal, Amen!?

It's already been settled in a legal court.

And through that revelation I come into **aggressive agreement** with God's covenant,

*…and I **reckon** myself heal**ed**,*

…and the devil cannot challenge that agreement, because it's legal, because of its integrity.

God's very integrity enforces its reality, amen!?

Now when I aggressively resist the enemy in agreement with God's covenant *he has to flee.* Amen!?

He has to flee.

I am legally resisting him, *and he has to flee.* Amen!?

And I'm not even wrestling and fighting with him directly myself, amen,

I just acknowledge and recognize* that he was defeated on that cross, and I address him with confidence and authority, and I stand firm, *steadfast in the faith, confessing my healing,

...but I don't even spend much time on addressing the devil, I'm not praying to him or giving him attention...

...he would just love to have the attention, and to have my focus...

...but my eyes are fixed on redemption realities, and my trust is in my Daddy, in Jesus my Healer, who enforces His blood covenant He made with me;

He enforces it with power!

The Holy Spirit of God Himself, who lives in me, and who loves me, quickens my mortal body, based on legal grounds,

...as I come into verbal faith agreement with God's covenant.

Amen!?

Hallelujah!

Chapter 10

"There is no fear in love..."

I want us to quickly go back to 1John 4.

Hey listen, verse 18 says:

1John 4:18

18 *"**there is no fear in love**"* Amen!?

God's perfect love, His marvelous, intense, perfect love for us casts out _all_ fear.

18 *"...**perfect love casts out fear,** because **fear involves torment**."*

*"...**fear involves torment**..."*

Are you being tormented by guilt and shame and fear?

God doesn't want you to continue to be tormented by the enemy.

God doesn't want His children living in constant fear, and in torment, over punishment, or sickness, or anything like that.

God doesn't want His children trapped in guilt and in shame, _in torment_.

Listen again to what He says:

1John 4:18

18 _"...But he who fears **has not been made perfect in love**"_

God wants to overwhelm you with His perfect love for you.

He wants to wash you with the knowledge of you being His very own child that He loves dearly.

He wants to wash away all that shame and fear from your life.

He wants to drive sin-consciousness and guilt out of your life entirely.

He wants to drive sin itself out of your life altogether.

God wants to deliver you absolutely.

God wants to set you totally totally free, through the knowledge of you being His child,

...and through the knowledge of His perfect love for you,

...and through the knowledge of His Sons' death on your behalf,

God wants to set you totally totally free, whether it's from sin, sickness, or anything!

He says there in 1 John:

Verse 19,

19 *"We love Him **because He first loved us.**"*

Could it be that you have no confidence towards God,

...that you are being tormented by fear and guilt and shame, **because you have not known,**

...or if you have known, **you have not believed, or fully embraced, the love God has *for you*?**

O God, we need a fresh revelation of the immense and perfect, wonderful, marvelous love of our Daddy,

...**we need a revelation of our blameless innocence before You,**

...**restored to us,**

...**by the blood of Jesus!**

Oh, we are so accepted in the Beloved!

Believe it!

Embrace it today!

Could it be that you are still living in bondage to sin, because your life is empty,

…because the void in your life, *designed to be filled by God's love alone,* has not been filled,

…even though you have been trying to fill it, with everything else, that cannot fulfill you?

Do you not yet know that what this natural world, what flesh has to offer, cannot fulfill you?

…it ends up being empty, it falls short!

You cannot **full-fill** you.

Not even living for your selfish self…

Money cannot **full-fill** you.

Things cannot **full-fill** you.

Prestige cannot **full-fill** you.

Fame cannot **full-fill** you.

Fun cannot **full-fill** you.

Sex cannot **full-fill** you.

Drugs, the latest thrill, cannot **full-fill** you.

Not even your spouse, not even your lover can **full-fill** you.

Only God can friend, only the love of God can!

Only embracing God's love for you, *fully*, can do that friend!

Could it be that even though you are a Christian, you are still trapped in bondage, <u>**because you are deceived,**</u>

...**because you have remained deliberately oblivious, ignorant,** concerning the knowledge of sonship,

...concerning the knowledge of you being a child of God **now,**

...concerning the knowledge of you being totally a new creation **already,**

...concerning the knowledge that **you have dominion** over sin and guilt and shame and fear,

...concerning the knowledge that *sin does not have to have dominion over you,*

...concerning the knowledge that you are **already** a partaker of the Divine nature,

…that the love of God has **already** been planted into your heart **in full measure?**

Hosea 4:6 says,

6 *"My people are destroyed **for lack of knowledge,** <u>**because you have rejected knowledge**</u>…"*

Listen you don't have to continue to live **as a mere man** anymore,

…you can enter into a most satisfying, fulfilled, love relationship with God, *in total innocence and blamelessness,*

…**by knowing, <u>and believing</u>, that *you* <u>are</u> accepted in the Beloved,**

…**by knowing, <u>and believing</u>, the love God has for *you*,**

…**by knowing, <u>and believing</u>, that *you* <u>belong</u> in *your Daddy's arms,***

…**by knowing, <u>and believing</u>, that *you* <u>are</u> a new creation,**

…<u>**as He is, so are *you*,**</u> in this world.

You don't have to live **as a mere man** anymore!

Isn't that good news?

As you begin to abide in Him **through faith**,

...and **as you begin to allow His Word; His Truth, to abide in you, through faith**,

"God is at work within you, both to will and to do of His good pleasure."

Jesus will not disappoint you.

God's love will never disappoint you.

That love will bring you into **the full experience** of all these things,

...*the deep things of the heart of God,*

...**intimate relationship** with God.

As you begin to fully embrace and enjoy the height and the depth, the length and the breath of His love,

...**it will make the experience of all these other things a reality**;

...*freedom from sin, freedom from guilt and shame and fear,*

...*innocence and blamelessness* in the midst of a crooked and perverse generation

It is bound to make 1John 4:17 a reality:

17 *"As He is **so are we** in this world"*

It is bound to affect, permanently, in a positive way, your relationship with your fellow man.

It is bound to cause you to shine forth the light of life,

…walking in the love of God,

…ever witnessing to your fellow man about the love God has for you, and them as well.

2Corinthians 5:14 says,

14 *"For the love of Christ **constrains us**,"*

"…because we judge thus:"

*"…that **if One died for all, then all died**; "*

(*"**Of God are you in Christ Jesus**, who became to us wisdom from God – and righteousness and sanctification and redemption"* 1Corinthians 1:30

In the mind of God, we all, *the whole human race,* **died in Christ, and was raised, now legally to enjoy newness of life.** [Isaiah 66:7 & 8, Hosea 6:2.]

You can also go study Romans 4 verse 25 and chapter 5 from verse 6 onwards to understand this more fully.)

2Corinthians 5:15-21

15 *"and **He died <u>for all</u>, that those who live should live no longer for themselves, but for Him** who died for them and rose again."*

16 *"**Therefore, from now on, we regard <u>no one</u> according to the flesh.** (Even though we have known Christ according to the flesh, yet now we know Him thus no longer.)"*

17 *"So* (the conclusion is), *if anyone is in Christ,* **he is** *a new creation;* **old things (old realities)** *have passed away, behold all things have become new."*

When did this happen?

When Christ died and was raised!

18 *"**<u>Now</u> all these things** (these new realities) **are of God**, <u>who **has** reconciled us to Himself</u> through Jesus Christ, **and has given us the ministry of reconciliation."**

What is that ministry all about?

19 *"that is, that **God was reconciling <u>the whole world</u> to Himself in Christ, <u>not imputing their trespasses to them</u>**, <u>and so He has committed to us all, the word of reconciliation</u>."*

20 *"**Therefore we are ambassadors for Christ**, <u>as though God Himself were pleading through us</u>: **We implore everyone on Christ's behalf, <u>be</u> reconciled to God**,"*

155

21 *"**For He made Him who knew no sin, sin for us, that, in Him,** (in His work of redemption) **we might become the righteousness of God**."*

Based on this revelation, Gerald Sharp, a friend of mine wrote a profound song that I will only give the words to in this book:

Show me a man who can stand before God and not be ashamed of his life.

I am a man, I can stand before God; I'm no longer ashamed of my life.

For it's the life of Jesus, by the blood of Jesus

There's no other name under heaven by which we can be saved

Just the name of Jesus…

Show me a man who can stand before God and not be ashamed of his life.

You are a man, you can stand before God, don't be ashamed of your life.

Cause it's the life of Jesus, by the blood of Jesus

There's no other name under heaven by which you can be saved

Just the name of Jesus…

156

…You are a man, you can stand before God; don't be ashamed of your life.

It's the life of Jesus, by the blood of Jesus

There's no other name under heaven by which you will be saved

Just the name of Jesus…

…by the blood of Jesus

Just the name of Jesus…

…by the blood of Jesus

Again, Romans chapter 8 verses 1 & 2 reiterates,

1 "*…***There is therefore <u>now no condemnation to those</u> who are in Christ Jesus, <u>who live according to this revelation of the Spirit</u> and not according to the witness of the flesh**,"

2 *"for the law of the Spirit, of **life in Christ Jesus*** (the law of faith, the revelation of faith, the revelation of the New Covenant) ***has made me free*** *from the law of sin and death, (…of* the influence of guilt, shame, failure and sin; of separation from God, unable to approach Him)*"*

I have been set free from the power of it, the empty bondage, living the cycle of sin and guilt and shame and separation, hallelujah!

Chapter 11

For with the heart one believes

The Bible says in Romans 10:6-13

6 *"...the righteousness, **which is of faith,** speaks this way..."*

8 *"...it says '**The Word is near you, <u>even in your mouth</u> and in your heart**.'*

"This then is also the Word of faith that we preach:

9 *"that **if <u>you</u> confess with <u>your</u> mouth** (if you say the same thing with your mouth as God says about) the Lord Jesus* (and His work of redemption) *and believe in <u>your</u> heart that God has raised Him from the dead* (and that He has raised you up with Him at the same time, to newness of life, because you were in Him when He died, and you were also in Him when He was raised, **if you believe these things as reality**) <u>**you**</u> **will be saved** (rescued, made whole)."*

10 *"**For with the heart <u>one believes</u> to righteousness, <u>and with the mouth confession is made</u>** (coming into total agreement with God; coming to the right*

conclusion and verbalizing to yourself and others what you believe) *resulting in salvation*."

11 *"For the Scripture says; "**Whoever** believes on Him* (believes in Jesus, in His incarnation and His work of redemption; in the Father's message of love and eternal truth revealed there) *will not be put to shame.*"

13 *For* "<u>whoever</u> (anyone, everyone, <u>that</u> <u>includes *you*</u> who) *call* upon (who identify with) *the name of the Lord* (with His work of redemption) *shall be saved* (rescued, made whole)."

Hallelujah!

1John 1:9 says:

9 *"If we confess our sins* (not merely admitting to a sin committed, but instead, we *"confess"* or better yet, *"profess"* over our sin; in other words, we come into aggressive agreement with God over our sins; *over the fact that our sins have been dealt with and wiped away, and sin's power was broken over us on that cross,*

…we are no longer making excuses for it, *but we genuinely see our freedom from it,* and now wanting and demanding it to go, to be totally removed out of our lives),

He (God) *is faithful and just* (based on what Jesus legally did for us *and based on the fact that we now actually see and believe it*) <u>*to forgive us our sins,*</u>

<u>*...and to cleanse us from all unrighteousness.*</u>"

If this prayer expresses what is in your heart, you can express your heart by praying it if you want:

Lord Jesus, thank you for dying for my sin on the cross, that I may be set free and be made righteous.

Father God, thank you for forgiving my sin, blotting it out, and accepting me into blameless innocent fellowship with You.

Lord Jesus thank you that as faith is now awaked in my heart, *you come with that faith, and you come and set up residency and live in my heart.*

Be my leader in these things and my Lord by your Word and by your Spirit.

Thank you for sending the Holy Spirit of truth to me, imparting your truth to me, imparting Himself even, to live in me, *and changing me from the inside out.* Amen.

The Scriptures say in 1Corinthians 6:17 that,

17 *"He who is joined to the Lord is one spirit with Him"*

It also says in 2Corinthians 5:17 that,

17 *"If anyone is in Christ, **he is a new creation**, the old things* (what was true about your life, the old realities) ***have** pass**ed** away, behold **all things have become new**."* NKJV

If you want to grow in your fellowship with God, the Word of Truth, the Word of Redemption, the Gospel, must find its rightful place in your heart.

The apostle Peter said in 1Peter 2:2 & 3 that,

2 *"...like newborn infants,* (you must **earnestly desire**) *long for, the pure spiritual milk of the Word **that you may grow thereby**"*

3 *"if indeed you have tasted that the Lord is good"*

God has been real with you, *now be real with God.*

Do not play games with Him.

God has always meant business with you, *now you mean business with God.*

Mean business with His Word.

Treasure what He has to say in His Word, in your heart.

Live your life consistently by its truth and reality, <u>not just when you feel like it</u>.

Do not deceive yourself, truth is truth; you cannot escape the reality of truth!

Either it's reality, or not, and if it is reality, then you might as well live what it reveals about you, *without deceiving yourself and preferring to live a lie!*

In John 17, Jesus prayed for us, and this is what He prayed:

*"Father, the hour has come. Glorify Your Son, that Your Son also may glorify You, as **You have given Him authority over all flesh, <u>that He should give eternal life</u>** to the many You have given Him."*

("...to the many" ...to everyone, that means all of us, <u>**you**</u> included,)

<u>*"And this is eternal life, that they may KNOW You, the only true God, and Jesus Christ whom You have sent*</u>."

"I have manifested Your name to these (those who have received Him and believe in Him) *whom You have given Me out of the world. They were Yours, You gave them to Me"*

How?

Through Your Word,

*"... and **they have kept Your Word**."*

How did they keep it?

How do we keep it?

*"**For I have given them the words which You have given Me, and** they have received them"*

They believed them, treasured them and held fast to them, and that's how we were given to Jesus by the Father, that's how we became His disciples,

*"**They are not of the world, just as I am not of the world**."*

*"**Set them apart (cleanse them, draw them closer to yourself) by Your Truth. YOUR WORD IS TRUTH.**"* NKJV

He also said this in John 14, 15, 16:

*"If anyone loves Me, **he will keep** (believe, treasure, hold fast to, live by) **My Word**;"*

*"**and My Father will love him, and We will come to him, and make our home with him**."*

*"**Just as the Father has loved Me, I have also loved you**; "*

"…abide in My love."

*"**Abide in Me, and I in you.**"*

How?

By seeing His Truth, and treasuring His Word.

*"As the branch cannot bear fruit of itself, <u>unless it abides in the vine</u>, so **neither can you, unless you abide in Me**."*

"I am the vine, you are the branches;"

*"**He who abides in Me, and I in him, he bears much fruit**;"*

*"**By this My Father is glorified, that you bear much fruit**;"*

"…and so prove to be My disciples."

*"**You are my friends if you <u>do</u> whatever I command You** (if you believe what I have so strongly revealed to you as truth!)"*

*"**If you <u>keep</u>** (believe, treasure, and live) **my commandments** (My emphatic Truth; My reality revealed)**, <u>you will abide in My love</u>**,"*

*"... **just as I have kept** (believed, treasured, and lived) **My Father's commandments** (His emphatic Truth; His reality revealed)**, and abide in His love**."*

*"**This is My commandment** (based on the Truth and reality I revealed to you,) **<u>that you love one another just as I have loved you</u>**."*

*"**<u>This I command you</u> (this is Truth's conclusion,) <u>that you love one another</u>**."*
NKJV

Jesus revealed that love includes everyone, all people, no matter what race, but especially other Christian brothers and sisters, it is what we were created for. It is His reality, and truth's conclusion about us, about our design.

...we are His image and likeness.

That is why the strong language. To live outside of such a command is to ignore reality, and to live outside of truth; *it is to deceive oneself and live a lie!*

In another place He made it clear that, to love means, to love everyone, when He said, *"Love your enemies,"*

... that means people you used to hate for any reason, or that hated you, or might still hate you, for whatever reason.

If you ask God, He will lead you and help you get connected, and become friends with other Christians who believe and live by these new creation realities.

Trust me we all need fellowship with people like that.

We need to stay in fellowship with each other in these realities, least we again, drift away from it.

It is easy to drift away from truth and ignore it again if you don't have others in your life *that speak the same thing and can help you keep your thinking straight.*

Ask Daddy to connect you with Christians that know these truths, and that know what it is to be immersed in the Holy Spirit.

Christians that know how to flow in the Holy Spirit and know how to operate in the gifts of the Spirit, and can speak in other tongues, and prophecy and do miracles, just like the believers did in the book of Acts.

They will share with you, and help you get immersed in redemption truth, and in the Holy Spirit.

They will love you and be there for you, just like the real family of God should be for each other, and they will encourage you as

167

you grow spiritually *into the full manifestation of this new creation you already are.*

Father, we thank you for your Word.

We thank you that your Word is alive, and that it's Truth!

…when Jesus prayed that You would not take us out of the world, but keep us from the evil one, He prayed,

"Father, sanctify them, set them apart, with your Truth, your Word is Truth."

I thank you that we experience, even as we listen to your Word, even as we speak your Word, we experience, Father, that your Word *lifts us up beyond the reach of our enemy;*

You *separate us from* the evil one, *beyond the reach of darkness* Father.

Father, You've placed a light within us that cannot be challenged by this world's darkness *because there's more virtue in this light than what there is in this world's darkness,*

…and we're challenged within our spirits as we face the future, Father, *to arise and shine for our light has come,* and, O Father, that light is not just some nice little religious thought, *it's the revelation of Your covenant with us that shines forth into our hearts.*

…It is the God who said, *"Let light shine out of darkness,"* that shone into our hearts *the revelation of that covenant, in the face of Christ.*

Father, in <u>this</u> *we've come to know Your love* and the love of Christ, *and we believe in it,* and that love *is perfected in us.*

…Father, and we would endeavor *to treasure that perfect love* in our spirits that perfectly cleanses our conscience, that perfectly releases us from guilt; *that presents us innocent.*

Thank you Papa!

…And Daddy, as we recognize *that **reality**,* we are challenged to no longer consider any man from a human point of view, we are challenged to see them *as having already died in Christ,*

…and if any man died in Christ *he is a new creature,* the old realities have passed away, *look now, behold, everything has become new*

…We are challenged to preach to them the gospel, t*he good news that, "God, in Christ Jesus, reconciled the world to himself. Therefore, come now and be reconciled to your Daddy, come now and legally enter into your righteousness, come and enjoy freely, blameless innocence with Him."*

We honor You God!

Bless Your holy name Father!

We worship Your Majesty!

Hallelujah!

We love you Daddy God. Amen.

In closing, I urge you to get yourself a copy of *"The Mirror Bible"* available online at: www.friendsofthemirror.com or at www.amazon.com and several other book sellers.

If you want me or someone a part of our team to come to where you are, anywhere in the world, and give a talk or teach you and some of your friends about the gospel message, and these redemption realities, simply contact us at www.livingwordintl.com …or you can always find me on www.facebook.com

I pray that God may richly bless you in your life, and that you would prosper and be in health *even as your soul prospers in this new intimate, blameless, innocent, relationship with God which He has brought you into.*

If you have been helped, or your perspective on life has changed because of reading this book, please get in touch with me and let me know.

I would love to share your joy so that my joy in writing this book may be full.

For this reason, I bow my knees to the Father of our Lord Jesus Christ,

from whom the whole family in Heaven and earth is named,

that He would grant you, according to the riches of His grace,
to be strengthened with might through His Spirit in your inner man,
(His Spirit uses His Word to do this)

that Christ may dwell in your
hearts through faith;

that you may be rooted and
grounded in Love,
and may be able to comprehend
together with all the saints
the width, depth, and height of it
to intimately know the love of
Christ
which surpasses knowledge;

so that you may be filled
with all the fullness of God.
- Ephesians 3:14-19

About the Author

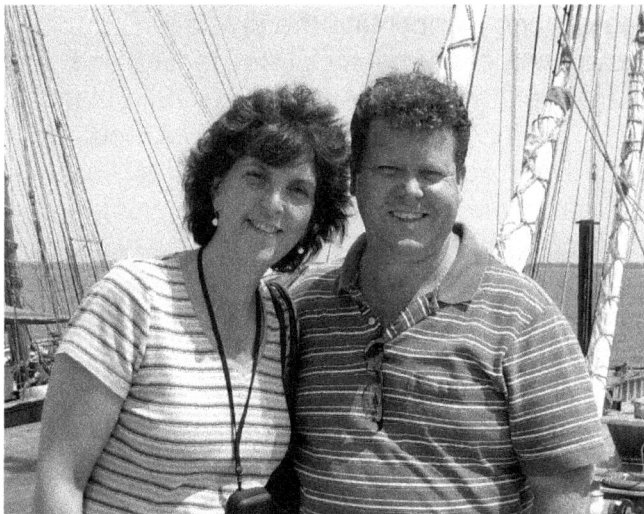

Rudi & Carmen Louw together oversee and pastor a church: Living Word International.

They also travel and minister both locally and internationally.

Rudi was born and raised in the country of South Africa while Carmen grew up in Cortland, New York.

They function in the ministry of reconciliation (2Corinthians 5:18-21) and flow strongly in the gifts of the Holy Spirit and His anointing to teach, preach, prophecy, heal and whatever is needed to touch people's lives with the reality of God's love and power.

God has given them keen insight into what He has to say to mankind in the work of redemption, concerning the revelation of, and restoration of, humanity's true identity, and therefore they emphasize THE GOSPEL; IN CHRIST REALITIES; the GRACE of God; the WORD OF RIGHTEOUSNESS and all such eternal truths essential to salvation and living of the CHRIST-LIFE.

They have been granted this wisdom and revelation into the knowledge of God, by the resurrected Spirit of Jesus Christ, to establish and strengthen believers in the faith of God, and to activate them in ministering to others.

Not only are people set free from the poison and bondage of sin, condemnation and all kinds of intimidation, (upheld, strengthened and reinforced by age old religious ideas born out of ignorance,) but many are brought into a closer more intimate relationship with Father God, as Daddy, through accurate teaching, and unveiling of the gospel message, prophetic words, healings and miracles.

Rudi & Carmen are closely knitted together in friendship with several other effective Christians, church fellowships, and groups of believers who share the same revelation and passion.

174

www.ingramcontent.com/pod-product-compliance
Lightning Source LLC
Chambersburg PA
CBHW051834090426
42736CB00011B/1795

* 9 7 8 0 6 1 5 8 3 5 3 1 0 *